IN SEARCH OF

GOLD

FREDERICK J. SMITH

In this you greatly rejoice, though now for a little while you may have had to suffer grief in all kinds of trials. These have come so that your faith — of greater worth than gold, which perishes even though refined by fire — may be proved genuine and may result in praise, glory and honour . . .

1 Peter 1:6 and 7

Printed by Wright's (Sandbach) Ltd.
Cover Design by Catherine S. Cheetham

Foreword

If God were to take you and give you a glimpse of Gwen Gold in the presence of her Lord, I am sure her face would be lit up with smiles and crinkles at the corners of her eyes. When Gwen told her humorous missionary stories, or one of her endless supply of jokes, or simply worshipped the Lord in song or in prayer her whole face was involved. Gwen was the kind of person whose faith, joy and fun were infectious. She would often say, "My face is so funny everybody laughs."

As I got to know Gwen over the years, not only as a friend but also in my capacity as a Director of the Central Asian Mission, the society with whom her close friend Valerie Luff works, I found a deeply God-conscious person, one who had clearly proved God's sufficiency in every area of her life. She was very human with a typical Cockney directness that sometimes got her into trouble with some of her colleagues and friends. She often commented, "When He has tried me I shall come forth as gold." As the years went by, the evidence of gold — God's sanctifying power — grew in Gwen's life, and to the end she was a blessing and a challenge.

It was a great joy for my friend, Jean Mutimer,

and me to visit Nigeria in November 1984. A close bond, particularly in prayer, had grown up between Gwen, Valerie, Jean and myself. One of our main reasons for visiting Nigeria was to see Gwen and some of the work in which Qua Iboe Fellowship were involved.

Our stay with Gwen was a memorable time; her unstinting dedication as a servant of Jesus Christ, clear love for the people, and theirs for her, was a tremendous inspiration.

During the time we were with Gwen in Nigeria there were moments when we were conscious of an inward struggle, perhaps a weariness. The tragic death of her nephew some weeks before, the increasing pressures of work at the clinic, her deep burden for the Qua Iboe Church, and the longing to see a harvest of souls in Kanyehu sometimes seemed almost more than she could bear.

After a few days together staying with friends in Kaduna, she was eager to return to Kanyehu. Her usual sense of humour was clearly to the fore as she said goodbye. Some humorous remark made us all laugh as she drove off, waving. A few hours later the battle was over, Gwen was in the presence of her Lord.

I commend this book to you. It gives a deep insight into the work of the Qua Iboe Fellowship, and in particular to one of its workers. It demonstrates what God can do in an ordinary person's life totally dedicated to Him. Its thrilling descriptions of her personal experiences and her encounters with danger will cause you to want to know more about the God she loved and served. As you read this book will you consider your commitment to Jesus Christ and your involvement in World Mission?

PATRICIA F. COOK
Executive Director Central Asian Mission

Preface

Gwen Gold was not one of those saints whose lives, when written, leave the everyday Christian gasping in wonder, and not a little despondent. She was an ordinary cockney girl, down to earth, sharing our prejudices and follies. God in His wisdom did not change her base metal, but He did beautifully refine it. The end result was a woman with whom we can readily identify, giving us hope that the same Holy Spirit who worked in her so fully may yet do so in us.

Throughout the writing of this short book I have been conscious of Gwen as the friend we knew so well, full of laughter and fun. There is no way those twinkling eyes would allow me to over-state the case. Gwen would have said, "Come off it, Fred, who are you kidding?" If some of my readers would have preferred only the icing I am quite sure Gwen would not.

The story has another dimension, that of the work of God along the Benue river basin. The south bank witnessed some dramatic spiritual growth while the north stayed relatively barren. Perhaps this latter area awaits an opening of the windows of heaven such as will only come when we bring all the tithes into the storehouse; when we give ourselves to prayer and fasting. The gates of hell seem doubly barred to the gospel, rusted of hinge and well defended over many generations. But the promise remains, given by the Lord Himself, "I will build my church."

Some Nigerian friends would have preferred me to use the name Toto-Umaisha District instead of Bassa, as I have throughout this book. However, not only would the first term be clumsy, it would also convey nothing to the great majority of people in the United Kingdom. I would therefore ask that the name Bassa be accepted, whilst recognising that many people other than Bassas live in the area.

I wish to thank Lorna Baird for her help and all those of the Qua Iboe Fellowship who supplied me with information, in particular, Léon Griffiths. My thanks are also due to Katy Barrett, Liz Baker and Christine Price for typing the manuscript.

FRED SMITH
Chippenham, Wilts.

WHEN HE HAS TRIED ME

Where others pass, and passing see but mire,
His knowing eye detects a richer vein, a trace of
    promise.
Stooping, He works to sift and wash and sift again,
Till earth is laid aside and precious dust lies
    safely in His hand.

This now makes but commencement of His work
For fire alone can melt the inner core where lurks
    the dross of ages.
And He, His purpose well resolved, will fan the
    flame's white glow,
Skim, fan and skim again, in search of that blest
    image all His own.

At last His perfect dealings are complete;
Before His joyous gaze the one beloved shines clear
    with that same light.
This new creation, now refined, is homeward
    gently borne,
And set among the precious trophies of His grace.

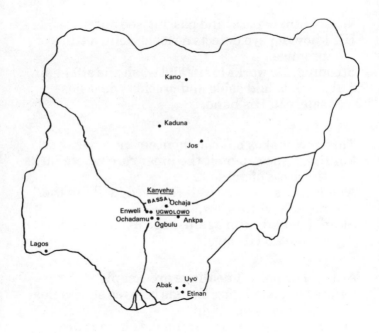

Map of Nigeria on which some places are shown where Gwen Gold worked as a missionary nurse.

Contents

CHAPTER 1

Glint of Promise

It was a chill November day when the two small girls in a drab London suburb decided to brighten the world a little. The mingled excitement and fear they felt served both to urge and yet to warn of danger. Had they not had each other to dare and challenge perhaps the moment would have passed. Perhaps then this story would not have been told.

Gwen Gold, even smaller than her seven years would warrant, and her older sister decided to have an indoor fireworks party of their own. The young fingers, trembling with the matches, eventually managed to light one of the innocent-looking packages and their world exploded into a flaming terror. Within seconds the cloth on the mantleshelf was ablaze, flames licked at the wallpaper, curling it away to cascade in deadly flakes to the floor. Smoke billowed menacingly around the terrified children causing their frantic cries to be choked by coughing as small lungs fought for air. It was then, happily, that a neighbour was alerted, the children led out of the house and the fire extinguished; but in the relief at the averting of a major tragedy no one realised that little Gwen had suffered deep shock which would affect her for years to come.

Very soon Gwen became ill, and a series of visits to puzzled doctors ensued without a clue to the cause. At last she was admitted to hospital where diabetes was diagnosed to have developed as a direct result of the shock. Six months in the children's ward meant that she fell behind in her formal schooling; but as she loved to read any book that came to hand her knowledge and vocabulary grew, well-compensating for any loss in other realms.

At least one of the nurses who attended the inquisitive child was a Christian. She joined in the campaign to supply the avid reader with suitable books. One Christian story-book intrigued Gwen particularly and, as she came to the last page, she found a place where a simple challenge was addressed to the reader to give her heart to the Lord Jesus Christ. Gwen, at eight years of age, solemnly wrote her name into the appropriate places of John 3:16; and promptly forgot all about it. But the Lord most certainly did not.

At fourteen years of age she had a remarkable and spontaneous cure. A panel of doctors was called in to examine this curiosity and was quite astonished at what it discovered. Some experts questioned whether she had actually been a diabetic in the first place, until it was pointed out that if not, the amount of insulin she had been given over a seven-year period would certainly have killed her.

By now World War II was at full pitch and the trauma of twice-daily visits to the hospital for injections was replaced by air raids, bombs and shelters. At least in this trouble she was not alone but shared the common stress of all her school friends. Her cockney sense of humour showed her the funny side of most situations, and she began to develop that exuberant chuckle which was to help her, and many another, in later years.

Wholly unknown to Gwen, there was another war opening up in a place called Bassa, north of the Nigerian river Benue. Earnest prayer was being made for a people known only by name, and a bridgehead was being established by a few intrepid pioneers who had a vision and a commission to make Christ known among the animists of the Benue basin. Human intellect would not have seen the link between the little girl of the London streets and the mighty spiritual forces being drawn up in far-away Nigeria. Nor could it be imagined that this bright-eyed lass would play a leading role in God's purpose for His Kingdom there.

Gwen was, in fact, quite a fearful child, which, together with her diminutive form, did not go unnoticed by the school bullies who loved to taunt and tease her. On one occasion they had snatched her hat and were having a whale of a time throwing it from one to another, while Gwen tried vainly to retrieve it. When finally they tired of the sport, Gwen went home crying. Outside her friend's home, and still sobbing, a scornful call came from the mother inside, "Who is that crying out there?"

"Not me!" replied Gwen's friend indignantly.

Gwen checked her tears, took a deep breath and resolved never again to be caught out in weakness. Within a few days the bullies soon learnt to their cost that the kitten had become a tigress.

In fact her new found boldness lasted all her life and was later sanctified in many dangerous situations. But it was much more complex than just a change of stance; she was actually afraid of being afraid, lest her weakness return to overwhelm her. When she went at last to Nigeria, her closest friend, Valerie Luff, made her promise not to indulge in any false heroics if she were attacked, or held up by bandits.

"Just hand over the cash, dear, don't whack them with your bicycle pump!"

Further steel was forged into Gwen's character in her teens by a period with the Women's Royal Naval Service where discipline and obedience were cardinal virtues. These played a decisive role in her later years when she had to listen carefully to some special orders and show an extraordinary degree of self-discipline in carrying them to completion.

Whether Gwen's years of experience as a patient had an effect on her choice of vocation, it is hard to say, but after the W.R.N.S. she began nursing training at the King George V Hospital, Ilford. Once more, however, illness was to interrupt her plans. This time it was her mother, who was found to be terminally ill, for whom the great personal sacrifice was willingly made. Gwen gave up her training and the friends she had made at the hospital and returned home. There could be no certainty when, or whether, she would be able to pick up the broken threads again.

Those who have witnessed the innumerable occasions when Gwen lovingly nursed and tended the needs of complete strangers, without thought for her rest, or food, will have no difficulty in imagining how tenderly she cared for her own. When at last her mother slipped out of her world of pain and distress, Gwen found herself unable to cry. After the weeks of closeness to her mother, the final days, the funeral and the family's joint sorrow, all she could feel was hollow, empty, numb. Days ran into weeks, with her emotions in a condition of total drought, until suddenly, without warning, the floodgates opened and the healing stream of tears flowed, and flowed. Her family, at first relieved at the break in tension, were later concerned by the sheer volume of weeping their youngest sister produced; but eventually the storm subsided and the sunny smile once more became a regular cheering aspect of her daily life.

An opening came for Gwen to take up her training again, this time at the West Middlesex Hospital. As she strode into the imposing building on her first day, staunchly hiding her rising panic, she could not know that it would be here that a key event in her life would take place.

The leader of the Christian Fellowship at the hospital was a girl named Margaret Woodward. She and Gwen were cast together quite often on the wards and it was natural that spiritual matters should be discussed at times. Gwen became intrigued with some of the things she heard, and went occasionally to the N.C.F. meetings. She was no fool, and above all she had no wish to fool herself. There was no doubt in her mind that there was a grand reality in these Christian girls, that she did not have what they had, and that she wanted it.

In Margaret's room, one evening, Gwen asked some searching questions about the Lord Jesus and her own relationship with Him. As Margaret tried her best to furnish answers, so the light of truth dawned upon the young nurse's soul and she committed herself to Him who had paid the supreme penalty for her sins on Calvary's cross. She left that room aglow with the new life of Christ burning within and a joy far surpassing anything she had known before.

Joining Syon Mission Church, Brentford, she enjoyed the fellowship and teaching, growing in her faith and understanding of God's Word. But she was not the type to be content to sit for ever in the pew; she must put into practice the scriptural lessons, or they would be merely a beautiful theory.

Once her general and midwifery training were completed she had the chance to live out her Christian principles in the rough and tumble of district nursing around the West Ham streets and in the Hackney Maternity Hospital. It was during this time that she became conscious of a growing desire to serve the Lord in Nigeria. What she had heard and read of the vast need and the tremendous opportunities, not only for nursing skills but also for sharing faith with a people eager for the Word of God, made her long to help fill such a vital gap. She sought the Lord for direction and assurance of her calling and He led her to Lebanon Bible College. Graduates of this institute were naturally dubbed 'cedars'. True Gwen could hardly qualify in stature as much more than a shrub, but in character she was well on her way already to being a sturdy tree planted by the Lord.

By no means unaware of the fine young men at college she considered the possibility of one, or other, joining her in the service she envisaged in Nigeria; and the more she considered, the better she liked the idea. She took the matter to the Lord.

"Father, you have said, 'It is not good for man to be alone,' so this must be true of woman. Would you please call one of these men to Qua Iboe — and to me?"

She waited, prayed and waited but no-one offered to accompany her. On the last day of the last term she was puzzling over this when she suddenly realised that the Lord had pointed out right from the start how things would be. With a

18

chuckling appreciation that the joke was on her, she turned to the 'Daily Light' page for September 30th, the day on which she had first come to the college, it read: "When He has tried me I shall come forth as gold."

"That settles it then," she laughed aloud. "Thank you Father."

There can be no doubt that, in common with most people, she felt the pang of loneliness often after this, but the pain was not overwhelming now that her Father had shown her His will in the way she could best appreciate — kindly humour.

Leaning over the rail of the Elder Dempster ship, Gwen strained to get her first glimpse of the African coastline. Although she had studied every scrap of information she could find about Africa, and Nigeria in particular, she was aware of a vague fear expressing itself in a whole series of questions hammering at her heart: What would this vast land demand of her in sacrifice and dedication? Would she be able to cope with the physical and spiritual pressures? Could she last out the course, or would she soon be on her way back to London, a spiritual failure? After all, to her certain knowledge, others, whose Christian lives had seemed so strong at home, had been completely crushed by the demands of Africa. Who was she to imagine herself more capable, more spiritual?

As the fear rose to become almost tangible, so her prayers became more urgent, more desperate. There could be no bluffing, no shrugging of the shoulders. Here reality was stark, and faith would be exposed to the raw elements of forces far more vicious than she had yet encountered. Only those who have ventured to the far edge of faith and cast themselves out into the unknown upon Christ can begin to appreciate what Gethsemane means.

Until now the battle had been distant and its noise a thrilling challenge to young enthusiasm, but the clash of earnest deadly warfare was just over the hill and the new recruit could not be shielded from head-on conflict. She returned to her cabin and sought the comfort and strength that only her Lord could supply. Like many before and since she was learning the lessons of victory through submission.

She was, of course, not alone. That Christ had promised, "Go . . . I am with you always," was a fact; the full significance of which was just beginning to dawn in a certain consciousness of His delightful presence right here on this ship. But there was another comfort. She was not alone; she was part of a team of people stretching back before her birth and forward into the future. Some would work with her in Nigeria, some at home. Some had already completed their part; others had yet to be called.

CHAPTER 2

Beyond the Benue

Within sight of the River Benue, on its northern bank, lie three graves. A visitor to the area might be astonished to read the dates and inscriptions: "Stanley Kemp-Welch 1909." "Margaret Chapel Young 1913." "Ruby Stewart 1914." These were part of a pioneer team with the Sudan United Mission who began work on the Lucy Memorial Freed Slaves' Home at Umaisha in 1908. By the time the Home was operational there were one hundred and eighty-two children in care; all of whom had been liberated, but were now either orphaned or separated from their parents. As doctors tended the needs of these children, it was not long before folk from the surrounding villages brought their sick also, and the influence of the gospel began to be felt among the Bassa and Igbirra peoples.

On Sunday afternoons one, or more, of the staff would go into Umaisha town to hold a service. In 1910, Dr. and Mrs. Alexander reported on a service they conducted; "A number of people: about two hundred, gathered and listened most attentively. They began with a Hausa hymn. A beginning has also been made in three of the Bassa villages around here."

Stanley Kemp-Welch died after only four months in Nigeria; one of many who were required to lay down their lives almost before they could settle to the work. Margaret Chapel Young died in childbirth. Sleeping sickness became a scourge among the children and staff of the home and by 1918 the site at Umaisha was abandoned in favour of a healthier area.

Thus the struggle for Bassa, begun at such cost, lapsed for sixteen years. By 1934 a new set of visionaries, drawn by their Lord, lifted up their eyes towards the Benue and the people still waiting in darkness for the light of the glorious gospel of Christ to make its full impact.

While eight-year-old Gwen Gold was reading her first Christian story book in a London hospital, Herbert Dickson, Eddie Dornan and Jim Westgarth of the Qua Iboe Mission were setting off from Igala in an ancient Rover car to Oguma, which is south of the Benue, on the border between the Igala and Bassa areas. The first impressions were of a great need and a wide open door to the gospel, together with an inner assurance that the Holy Spirit was directing them to take up this challenge.

It was on their second visit to Oguma that a special feature of the area came to light. A great crowd had gathered and Herbert Dickson began to preach the Word of God to them, using as his interpreter a young Bassa man named Amodu. After a short time a section of the crowd began to murmer dissent. Dickson stopped.

"What's the trouble, Amodu?" he asked.

"Some of the people are angry, sir," Amodu replied. "They say you are speaking only to the Bassas, not to the Igbirras."

"Oh! What shall we do then? Can you speak Igbirra as well as Bassa and English?"

"Yes sir," Amodu grinned.

"Right then; I'll go along slowly to give you time to interpret."

Once more the message was taken up and the versatile lad followed each sentence fluently in two languages. But that was not the end of the matter, for soon another murmur arose, and this time from the Hausa speaking people.

"Why do you not speak to us in our tongue?" they complained. Herbert Dickson eyed his young friend.

"I can try, sir," Amodu laughed.

The whole crowd guessed what had been said and a roar of approving merriment preceded their settling down once more to hear this message too important to miss.

So the very unusual, and particularly difficult nature of the Bassa sector became evident. Unlike most of Nigeria, where in a given area one language predominates, here there were several language groups even in the same village or town. How were the emissaries of the Good News to weave their way through such a linguistic and cultural maze? Hausa, the language of huge areas of Northern Nigeria, was a possibility — especially since the Hausa Bible was already in print. Yet most of the local people knew only enough of this for trading; and virtually all stoutly refused to hear any important 'Word' in any but their own tongue.

Soon after this episode Mr. Westgarth toured north of the Benue, crossing the river at Ogba, in search of a site from which to reach these people. After a long and arduous trek of several days he returned to a place called Jinjere — fifteen miles east of the Niger and ten miles north of the Benue. Chief Alla was friendly and enthusiastic over the possibility of his town being chosen for the mission centre. His motives may not have exactly paralleled Westgarth's, but an agreement in principle was soon happily reached.

A message went out in three directions, to the United Kingdom, to the churches in the south, and to Igala:

> An urgent call for additional workers. It is quite evident that God has opened our way to these tribes. There is no time to lose, and we appeal for earnest prayer for the needed men.

Within a matter of weeks men were responding — converging on this new battleground to claim the area for Jesus. The cost for each one would be great. George Curry had been sent to open the work, and a Qua Iboe evangelist named Peter Asana, with his wife and little daughter were to share the burden with him. Amodu, now a convinced Christian himself, would act as interpreter. Also at that time two Igalas, Joshua Emeje and David Ocholi, were sent to live on the south side of the river to learn the language.

Herbert Dickson set aside nine days of his own demanding work at Adoru to introduce George Curry to Bassa in May 1936. In an old Morris car crammed with five people and a great deal of luggage, they set out from Idah with the few Christians there bidding them 'Godspeed'. After a sticky, bone-jarring hundred and sixteen miles they arrived at Ogba. There George took his first look at his new responsibility through the evening mist shrouding the river. As he strained to see the far shore, over a mile away across the silted water and sand banks, so the African night closed in, bearing a spiritual significance to the mind of the pioneer missionary.

Having procured carriers they set off the next day over the river and on towards Jinjere. Herbert went on ahead with the faster carriers, while George was left to urge on the slow ones. And they were still on the road as the sun began to set. Suddenly three of them threw down their burdens and refused to go any further. With Amodu's help George eventually managed to persuade them to retrieve their loads; and the party plodded on in the uneasy dusk, arriving at Jinjere in the dark to the throbbing of the welcoming drums.

Within a few weeks the rains were due, so work on three small one-roomed round houses of mud wall and thatch roof was hurried to completion. George occupied one, the teacher and his family another, and the young helpers the third. The Bassa children were very timid, unlike those of the Hausa or Nupe people. George tried in vain to coax them to the house where he hoped to make friends and from them to learn the rudiments of their language. The other children, however, made up for this by swarming around him from morning till night.

As George toured the area he discovered people everywhere willing to hear him. They were attracted by the gramophone and the large pictures he showed as he told the gospel stories. His journeys took him northward through a multitude of villages and towns but he was also conscious of the miles of unknown territory westward which needed to be reached. He wrote home at the time:

> It is going to be a difficult task. More and more I realise the need of the Holy Spirit for myself and for these people. I feel helpless in this vast country as I think of the great need.

By the time George was due leave it had become obvious that Jinjere, with its poor water supply, was not the best place on which to centre the work. Much to the grief of Chief Alla and his people, the Mission team moved twenty miles further along the river and five miles north to Kanyehu. Here the work was gradually established, and during the time George was at home Peter Asana reported a steady increase in attendance at the services.

The first real sign of a breakthrough came when two spirit worshippers, who had been attending services, refused to eat food offered to idols. The chief and his councillors arrived at Peter's door in great anger to complain at this breach of local custom. Peter heard them out, and then spent a long time talking to them of their idols and of the living God, till at last they retired, thoughtful, if not completely mollified.

A chief from a town five miles away sent four boys for instruction. By the end of 1938 thirteen people were attending the first enquirers' class — meeting for prayer and basic teaching in the Word on Thursday afternoons, in surroundings otherwise totally given over to animism. The Lord who stated, "I will build my church, and the gates of hell will not prevail against it," was once more at work. As with the first disciples, the building blocks looked somewhat unpromising to all but the eye of the Master Builder.

George Curry returned from leave with a new lantern projector. It was soon in use around the villages where Amodu and David Ocholi had already faithfully visited and begun to see results. The slides on 'The Life of Christ' proved invaluable as a teaching aid. No advertising was needed. As soon as it was dark and the large sheet-screen was erected, just about everyone who could run, walk, or crawl could be found jostling for a place of advantage to see the pictures.

The morning after the very first showing, at the village of Rikow, a young man came to enquire how he might follow "this Jesus". Later that day he took an immensely brave step of faith, in the awed presence of relatives and neighbours. Piling his idols and charms in the yard in front of his house he set them ablaze and, in defiance of all taboos, declared his total severance from spirit worship and his dependence upon Christ alone. While the Christians rejoiced, the relatives trembled, and the pagan society began to wonder what evil might follow these awful events.

As the weeks passed so the ones and twos came to the Saviour. One was the lead drummer in the Kanyehu 'band'. So when he rejected the pagan life he lost too his job at funerals, weddings and dances. A hard time for him was to follow, yet he was never to waver in his faith. Another, Iyese, defied all family pressures by burning her idols, and was soon severely tested when her son was killed by a baboon. Naturally she was blamed — the spirits having taken revenge on her in the most potent way possible. She was therefore constantly urged to make the appropriate sacrifice to ward off any further calamity to her family. But she stoutly refused, saying simply, "I am following Jesus." She even withstood the subtle temptation to pay someone else to sacrifice on her behalf.

Not all converts were consistent in their newfound faith. A man, who had made a bold profession of trust in Christ and had burnt his charms, was walking home one day at noon when he saw a deadly night adder on the path ahead. This phenomenon was considered a ghastly omen of impending doom requiring urgent consultation with the spirit medium. Only those who have spent their lives under such threats can appreciate the magnitude of the terror which must have struck this man's heart. In dreadful fear he returned to his old ways, making the appropriate sacrifice at the spirit shrine.

By the end of 1939, as the horrors of war were sweeping Europe and the world into chaos, Bassa too faced its challenges. Evangelist Peter Asana was forced to leave because of his wife's illness and return to his home in the south. But others from his tribe came to take his place. And in August 1940 George Curry was joined by Archie MacLellan. Then as the austerities of war began to bite in the homeland, it was not long before the effect was felt in Nigeria, forcing a number of normal commodities off the market. So while Gwen Gold was learning to cope with rationing in London, the team of workers in Bassa was finding it necessary to turn from imported foods to make greater use of local produce.

Despite privations and considerable opposition to the church's development, as well as difficulty in persuading parents to send their children to school, the work progressed steadily. Through faithful trekking and constant preaching a number of villages were opening up to the truth of the gospel. Tiny church buildings were blossoming in many places, and primitive schools were started, staffed by Nigerian teachers whose gifts often included fluency in five languages. Soon after his introduction to the work, Archie MacLellan wrote:

> Thirty Bassa people attended this afternoon's service at Kanyehu. I notice a greater equality between the sexes; men think highly of their women, often shaking hands with them. They are greatly attached to their homes. Islam has not impressed itself much upon them yet. As I

make contact with the Bassa people I become greatly
drawn to them. It would seem to me that the best way to
meet the needs of these villages is to have a travelling
Bassa evangelist.

Archie trekked through the area to Shafan and
Toto. From Toto he went west, visiting five towns;
returned to Toto and proceeded eastward as far as
the Gwari tribe amongst whom the Sudan Interior
Mission was working. Hoping for some refreshment and fellowship, he followed the directions
given by the local people to the S.I.M. Mission sta-
tion. After cycling for miles in the blazing sun he
had to give up his quest — to learn later that the
house he sought was in a different direction. By the
time he reached the main town of Nasarawa he had
preached the Good News in many places, to seven
language groups, and to Muslims and animists
alike.

The work in Bassa had been going on for twenty
years by the time Gwen Gold had settled into her
first situation at Ugwolawo in the Igala area of
Nigeria. Viewed in the perspective of so short a
time and so deprived a place, there was much to
encourage the mission and Nigerian church. A considerable number of villages now had their own
church building with a congregation ranging from
a few young people, to sixty or seventy. Several of
the bigger towns now had primary schools, taught
by local men and women as well as a few teachers
from further afield. Most of these were committed
Christians whose influence in the community and
church was considerable.

A succession of missionaries had helped to carry
the work forward despite many setbacks. Hymn
books, primers and Gospels were now in circulation in the Bassa language and a number of believers were so strong in their faith, clear in their wit-

ness and capable in the ministry of the Word as to be a challenge to all who knew them.

Discouragements there were also in good number. Often there simply was no-one available for work in Bassa; the area was left for long periods at a time without help, or one missionary might be sent for too short a time to become adequately accepted, or useful to the young church. Some Nigerians, thus grieved by what they had considered to be lack of concern on the part of the mission, became resentful or disaffected with the Christian faith. Others sowed seeds of discontent and still others turned to deliberate sin whilst attempting to continue in positions of authority in the church. All of this became cause for an ever-increasing concern in the sending churches of the United Kingdom and Nigeria. Earnest prayer was made by many for the area considered to be the hardest and least productive of all the Qua Iboe work.

CHAPTER 3

Igala Crucible

Like all new-comers to Africa, Gwen was intrigued by her novel surroundings. At Ugwolawo, working with Dorothy Bamber, she was highly amused at having to attend patients on the back verandah whilst waiting for the new dispensary to be completed. Not so funny was her first encounter with a very unfriendly spitting cobra whose venom just missed her eyes. Then there was her first tropical storm. She and Dorothy were both suffering the discomforts of a filarial rash, and were caring for a premature baby in the house, when the oppressive heat of the afternoon was disturbed by a rising wind. Shutters and doors were hastily fastened just before the tornado struck. Gwen describes the experience:

> We had just managed to close the doors when there was a terrifying noise. I thought the house had been struck by lightning but it was the corrugated roof of the verandah being torn off. It just floated away like paper. I thought the whole roof would go. We put the baby in what we thought was a safe place, and waited. When the wind died down the whole living room was flooded by torrential rain. Minutes after the rain ceased the Christians of the town came on the scene offering their sympathy and help. It did one's heart good to see their love

and concern. The chief came to "greet us for our suffering". Me thinks a little monotony would be welcome at times!

It was November 1957 before the new dispensary was opened officially by the Hon. P. S. Achimugu. Gwen was greatly impressed by this humble man of God whose life and witness as a judge and advisor to the Paramount Chief of Igala was without parallel. Just prior to the opening, Gwen had gone out to rescue twins whose mother had died. She brought them home in a basin on the back of her motorbike. When she reached Ugolwawo, one was already dead; the other she took to bed with her but he died during the night. So her great love for children was beginning to find expression, but not without pain.

A twelve-year-old boy crawled up the steep hill to the mission house. He had come over eleven miles with legs burnt to the bone and septic. He threw himself at Gwen's feet begging for help. There was no one to care for him and no money. Without hesitation he was taken in, treated, and lovingly cared for until he was completely restored to health.

It was while she was at Ugwolawo that Gwen had the first of many experiences of working entirely alone. Not only were there no other missionaries with her but she had no help with her daily chores. She was a very practical woman. She would "have a go" at most things, even invading the traditional male domains of mechanics and electronics. In her time she tackled such broken items as motor cycles, cars, water pumps, generators and a petrol-driven washing machine.

Her correspondence with friends and prayer partners fell behind as she struggled to keep both the dispensary and home going. In 1959 she wrote:

A midwifery case prevented me from attending any of the services on Easter Sunday, but several of the Christians came up to see me. The resurrection really means something to these folk who have come from the worship of idols. I was preaching to the lepers this week, and the wonder of the Easter message swept over me afresh as I related it to the patients and I just longed that they could appreciate it in the same way.

Though the work of the clinic was mostly routine there was plenty of excitement around the compound.

Two vipers were killed, an eagle took off a fully grown hen, and there was a cobra in the hen house! I very foolishly, when seeing a strange shape in the half-light of the early morning, went in to investigate. I am sure I broke all Olympic records when it uncoiled and revealed itself!

I see very little of my fellow missionaries. They do call in here but are usually on their way elsewhere, and once they have ascertained that I survive, continue on their journey — which gives little time, or opportunity, for fellowship. However, the Lord gives wonderful fellowship with Himself, which is more than adequate compensation.

Gwen's most frequent visitor was Kathleen Payne, whose work as advisor of the Q.I.M. primary schools often brought her through Ugwolawo. A warm friendship grew between these two Londoners, which was to endure, bringing mutual strength and refreshing. Remarkably, they were very different, but both of the independent mould. Off-duty weekends could mean time spent together completely relaxed; yet each character would hone the other to a fine awareness.

In her journeys to some of the nearby villages, Gwen became more conversant with the culture of the Igala people. Their friendliness and warm hospitality was a constant joy to her. She was greatly moved on many occasions by gifts of yam, eggs, hens or fruit brought as a token of appreciation felt at her visits. Sometimes it was a grateful patient, whose poverty was apparent, who would come with both hands outstretched, laden with a thank-offering.

Gwen hardly needed reminding of the value of her mission, but the recollection of an early experience and the recounting of it would sometimes serve as a timely prod. On trek and visiting one of the more remote villages, she began again to tell very simply the Good News — that the supreme sacrifice for sin had been made, and that there was therefore no need for further shedding of blood — when she had to stop. A murmur at the back of the crowd had become a heated exchange which could not be ignored. Through questioning her interpreter, Gwen learned its cause: "There is a man here, who says that he heard this word before, and the others are angry with him because he did not tell them."

Evidence of animism was everywhere, except where the gospel had had its purifying effect. Despite the natural interest she had in discovering the reasons for various customs, and the realisation that, had she been born here without the truth of God's Word to enlighten, she would be doing exactly the same as they were, Gwen always felt great sorrow in her heart over the bondage and suffering caused by spirit worship. Sometimes the concern she had for her patients would turn to indignation as the superstitions added extra terrible burdens to those already sick.

There was the child with epilepsy who had a fit and fell into the fire. No one would pull him out because of the 'demon' that possessed him. There was the woman whose children all died in their first year who was pronounced 'a witch'. When the next baby was due, no one would attend her. By the time Gwen saw her, both she and the baby were beyond saving.

But it was not until 1962 that Gwen was exposed to a personal threat from animism. Then she was briefly transferred to the isolated village of Enweli in Ibaji where paganism remained scarcely diluted by western influence. Describing her adventures in the Mission magazine under the title of 'His angels . . . to keep thee' she wrote:

> Many came to the Mission compound for medical help and, when asked to return during the following week, the women would answer, "It will be the time of the masqueraders then, and we are not allowed out. You must give me enough medicine now to last me . . ." On enquiry it seemed that the young men of the town, led by those dressed in gruesome ju-ju apparel, would not allow women outside — or even men who were strangers to the village. The penalty for disobedience was a sound beating with the sticks which the men carried. Children, too, were compelled to keep indoors.
>
> Just before the ceremony was due to begin a few elders from the village visited me and told me a little of what was to take place — a very little — they said that I should not go out. However, when I objected to this, in view of the treatment which one very sick woman in particular needed every day, reluctant permission was given.
>
> The festival began with a very noisy night. The drumming, shouting and singing kept us all awake. Seemingly this was the 'cleansing'. The masqueraders go to the houses of those discovered in some tribal offence (stealing being one of the greatest), and call out the offence committed for all to hear. Apparently this is one of the worst things that can happen to an Ibaji and keeps him so honest. (One boy had his 'sin' disclosed four years ago and ran to his farm, where he has lived ever since — sin without a Saviour!) The next day saw the 'occupation of the village'. I went to give the necessary injection to the aforementioned woman and found bamboo curtains in front of every door and window. Women and children crouched behind them, looking out in fear — and in won-

35

der too, as they saw Joseph, my helper, and me going about unhindered. The young men ran up and down the village shrieking like dervishes, and the ju-ju darted off into the houses off the main village street in the hope of catching an unwary woman or child. This continued for about five days. I was in the village every day and although angry mutterings were heard, and threatening looks were given, no action was taken. Indeed it gave occasion for witness. One man, a builder belonging to another tribe, asked Joseph how it was that we were not afraid. We testified to the One who would never leave or forsake, and found that we had attracted a bigger crowd of men than had the masqueraders!

However we did not try to provoke these evil men, and once our business was finished, we returned to the mission compound which, at times, was like a city of refuge. Children rushed to us in desperation and these men did not attempt on any occasion to cross the threshold of the mission territory.

On the Monday all was quiet, and I thought the festival was finished, so in the evening I decided to resume my usual habit of taking the dog to the stream. In the village there was a subdued air. Women were to be seen, but standing near the doorways of their houses. On reaching the end of the village, on the approach to the stream, I saw about a hundred men dressed in ju-ju apparel, stretched across the road. The first instinct was to return as quickly as possible in the direction from which I had come. However, I remembered that the previous days I had spoken in church on Matthew 10:28 — "Fear not them which are able to kill the body ..." — and I knew that if a retreat were made, the Word of God would be of little, or no effect in that village again.

To go on seemed impossible, especially with knees of jelly. A quick prayer was made, asking the Lord to make His presence known and to take away fear, and after this the step forward was taken. No words can describe how the Lord answered prayer. No courage was involved in walking through this group of evil men, for without fear there can be no courage — and the Lord had just taken away every atom of fear. One man jumped up and declared that I was a woman, the same as their own wives, and should be beaten. Even then the Lord kept me from fear. I was telling myself that it wasn't 'common sense', and no more it was — it was the Lord. No attempt was made to clear the path, but no one directly tried to block it, and so I continued to the stream.

Jonathan, my labourer, followed me and begged me to take the back road to the compound. At first I wondered if I should, for I had no desire to provoke these people. Then I asked Jonathan, "If I do this, will they not say that the devil has more power than God?"

Jonathan, very reluctantly, said, "Yes, Ma, that is what they will say."

"And what about you, Jonathan? Do you think the devil has more power than God?"

Poor Jonathan replied, "No, Ma, but he has more men on his side."

And what evidence of that there was.

However, in order to prove the Lord, it seemed necessary to go back through the crowd, and, again claiming His presence and asking Him to guard any reaction if the sticks should fall, I went back. As we came near we could hear the words, "The white woman is coming. Get ready for her." On reaching them, they got ready. They stepped back from the path, cleared the way for me, the majority of them giving me the familiar 'danyeku' — the bobbing of the knee — signifying respect. This was the 'exceeding abundant'.

There is always the danger in the telling of incidents like this, that glory may be given to the individual, but this individual knows that if it had not been for the grace of God she would have turned and fled, and so any glory belongs to Him and Him alone.

Although her time in Ibaji was short, Gwen decided to visit at least some of the many villages of the area, taking with her medicine and her Bible. She found that most people were eager for the former but often reluctant to 'hear' the message. However, like all her colleagues in the work, she believed in the ministry of health to the whole man. To preach the gospel to people whose sickness, or hunger, were foremost in their thoughts was not only unthinking but unworthy of the name of Him who had compassion on the multitudes. On

37

the other hand, to tend the present needs of the body only, was to ignore the deepest want of all, that of the soul.

During these treks she would take up residence in the local church or school, hold her clinics in the morning, visit homes in the afternoon and have meetings in the evening. By the end of the day she would collapse exhausted on to her camp bed and sleep soundly till dawn, despite the constant whine of an army of mosquitos intent on sucking her dry.

One such night she was wakened by vicious bites more reminiscent of scorpion than mosquitos. She leapt off the bed and was immediately assailed by a great deal more of the same. Driver ants! That most feared of all creatures by all others. Swarming in their millions over floor and walls and on up into the grass roof, they were intent on eating absolutely any and all flesh in their path, and missionaries were no exception. At that time of night, with no means of defence, Gwen's only course of action was retreat.

The alarm was raised and a good number of people came with lamps and torches to help her do a moonlight flit. With Gwen in the lead, clad only in her nightdress, the long procession made its way down the middle of the village to a new site judged to be far enough away from the ants at least for the rest of the night.

Once Gwen was settled again in her bed the vision of her walking along in her night attire suddenly made her laugh aloud. "Good thing my friends in London couldn't see me." True, it was becoming fashionable there to wear almost anything, but this might have been stretching it a bit far.

Back again at Ugwolawo she was responsible for leprosy clinics in several far-flung places and could often be seen in her Morris Traveller rattling over the corrugated laterite roads to the tinkling of medicine bottles and protestations of the over-loaded suspension units. Wherever she was, there was always a dog, either her own, or someone else's she was mothering, or both. It was not only that a dog was a help against loneliness, or a possible deterrent to any thief, but she really loved her dogs.

There was a succession of these animals: some very large and daunting, yet, to use her own description, 'soft as a penny bun'; others short of leg and long of body of the dachshund variety. She talked to them constantly, much to the astonish-ment of the Nigerians; was strict on discipline and manners and yet mingled all with large doses of tender loving care. They repaid her with total devotion and caused her many a hearty chuckle at their antics. Inevitably, in such a hostile climate, a dog rarely lived out its full life span. It would take Gwen a long time to get over losing her beloved Rusty, or whichever dog it happened to be, usually until she could take on another to replace him.

By 1964 a great deal of pressure was coming upon Gwen from several quarters. From home, news of her father's illness made her wonder if she should return to nurse him. Nigeria, four years into Independence, was changing rapidly. In some spheres there was considerable anti-white feeling and the political temperature was such that one could not help but speculate how much longer mis-sionaries would be welcomed. Sadly, too, Gwen was finding her spiritual life somewhat frayed around the edges; partly from overwork, partly from long periods alone, but also from some difficulties with the mission and some of its workers. Gwen, always outspoken, had on occasion encountered others with equally strong, but variant views.

At one stormy session it was suggested that funds from the medical work be diverted to help train students at Ankpa Bible College, Gwen swung into action:

> "Have you any idea of the abject poverty of some of my patients?" she challenged. "How can I demand payment from them for their medicines and treatment unless I know that it will only be used to improve facilities for them?"

Her determined chin thrust defiantly forward as she positively glowered at the senior missionaries who had dared to touch her medical work. This was Gwen — at her best and worst; she would fearlessly champion the weak; she was apt to see only absolutes.

Gwen was to say later of this period that it was a time when the Lord was trying to get through to her to knock off her rough edges. "It took Him a long time to do this, but," she would laugh with joy in her eyes, "He eventually pierced even my armour plating!"

So, under something of a personal cloud, Gwen returned to London and for the next two and a half years took leave of absence from the work. The Lord, though, had further plans for Gwen in Nigeria. Before her lay the most important part of her life as a missionary, and her Father knew she needed some time to consider, to be renewed by the Holy Spirit, and in every way fitted for the great task ahead.

CHAPTER 4

Black Lode

Since the pioneer years of George Curry and Archie MacLellan the work in Bassa had fluctuated between hopeful and disappointing. Right from the start the young church had suffered persecution from the animistic society out of which all its members had been snatched. Chiefs, priests and councillors soon recognised the danger to their whole way of life when their sons and daughters began to adopt 'this new way'.

The first baptismal service at Kanyehu signalled the fact that this was no passing phase, easily ignored, or absorbed into the culture. The crowd who watched Holobo, Daudu, Mejida, blind Holeji and the woman, Tukwuro, go down into the river proclaiming Jesus as their only Lord and Saviour, may not have understood all that was involved, but some certainly "wondered where to this thing would grow."

It was not long either before faith was to be tested. Helping him in the house George Curry had a young man, Omede, whom he had trained and brought with him from Igala. One Sunday before dawn Omede stepped out of his house on to a puff adder and was struck by a pair of two-inch-long messengers of death. No anti-venom was available and there was absolutely no way, humanly speaking, to save him. Within the hour Omede's condition was critical. Holeji came up with the answer: "If we have faith in God, Omede cannot die."

The Christians gathered around the lad in his room and prayed together the prayer of faith. Then they left him in their Father's care and went off to the church service. George Curry reported later:

> After the service was over, all with one accord hurried up the hill to the Mission. Great was the rejoicing to see Omede sitting up on his mat trying to smile. He was still far from well, but made rapid progress and in a few days was running around again as usual.

Iyese, who had stood the test when her son had been killed by a baboon, was now old and frail, but would still not miss a single chance to be at the services. One Sunday she staggered to church feeling so ill that she had to lie on the floor listening to the 'Word' which had become so precious. She was carried home, and within a few days it was obvious that she was dying. Five witch-doctors sat outside her house hurling insults and threats and mocking her faith in her 'Jesus'. She made no reply. When the Christians gathered they asked her if she wished to accept what these men said. Emphatically she shook her head.

"Do you still want to follow Jesus then, even in death?"

Iyese smiled weakly and nodded.

After her death her relatives claimed her body for pagan burial. Near midnight, as is the Bassa custom, they came in a great procession, throwing the body from one to another till they reached the place of burial. The Christians followed along, singing their hymns, while the chill wailing of the mourners rose and fell in stark contrast. Once buried, a great mound of stones was raised over her and a sacrifice was offered to the spirits, the blood poured as a libation over the stones. One of the Christians climbed the mound and planted a wooden cross right through the blood sacrifice. On the cross were three words: "Iyese, Jesus saves."

At the town of Sizi the preacher named Paul, who had been sent to them at their request, was doing a great work both there and in trekking to visit other places where there was no resident preacher. It was not long, however, before he encountered considerable opposition from the animistic hierarchy. This was to be expected, but what added an almost intolerable burden to his labours was that some of the Christians too resisted his leadership. On a visit to help Paul, George Curry had discovered his problems and was to experience one at first hand.

After dark two boys crept into the mission compound and presented themselves to Paul and George. They were very distressed. Their father had evicted them from the house because they had refused to eat meat offered to idols. They stayed the night, but the next day their father came with twenty men. His fury knew no bounds. For over an hour he screamed abuse at the preacher and missionary alike, before storming off. George had been completely unable to reason with him. The missionary wrote home:

> I was sorry to leave Paul behind in the midst of all this trouble but we had to push on . . . This is a hard place. We returned to Kanyehu with a heavy heart. After much thought we decided to set aside a whole week for intercession. We had three sessions each day with a special subject for prayer. As well as the work here we remem-

43

bered the church throughout the world. I gave a brief message on prayer at each meeting. We were conscious of God's presence during the week; now we had to look for the ingathering of souls in the days to come.

Archie MacLellan also wrote home regarding the joys and sorrows:

> At one town it can be said, as of some in scriptures, "Many walked no more with Him." A lad who was prepared to suffer persecution before has now gone back. He contracted smallpox and took offence at God. When he recovered he influenced some not to go to church and told the teacher, "If you find me in church again, take a knife and cut my throat!"
>
> We are busy building our second mission house at Toto. There is a strong Islamic influence in this town. We covet prayer for our efforts to proclaim Christ. The school at Oguma (on the south side of the River Benue) is still under our supervision, securing for us the opportunity to present the Word of God daily to thirty boys. A church has been built near the school and the teachers will help conduct the services.
>
> Last May (1944) we welcomed Elder Jacob Ahunanya of Oloko to Bassa to conduct a Bible course for the preachers. We have been encouraged by a recent moving of the Holy Spirit among the people at Kanyehu. An elderly man came out for the Lord, followed by a young man and woman. A few weeks later others came after the service saying, "We want to turn from paganism." Next day the wife of our headman also signified her desire to become a Christian.

For health reasons it was decided to transfer George Curry back to the south. On his return from home leave he went to Kanyehu to collect his belongings and share a final Sunday with the believers. In reminiscent mood he describes the scene in church that morning:

> On Sunday morning, 16th June, 1946, I sat in Kanyehu church after an absence of two years. I watched the congregation arriving; a few were already in their places.

Holeji, now totally blind, was in the front row. It is nine years since he, with four others, made a stand for Christ. He had gladdened our hearts when, almost sightless, he had offered to go out and preach. He went because there were so few to tell the Bassas about Christ. On foot he covered a large area where the Good News had never before (or since) been proclaimed.

Then there was Medjida, another of the five, a young man who had caused us many a heartache by his waywardness. We yet believe he will do great things for God.

Near the back sat Jimbe. In 1942 his young child died, and stricken with grief and bitterness, he left the church to return to his heathen worship. Now he has come back to seek that perfect peace only found in Christ.

Daudu and his wife came in. They are the only Christian couple in the district. Ahasaba, the wife, was dressed in a coloured garment with a neat head covering — a revolution in fashions — as the Bassa women wear only black and go bare-headed.

Presently Evangelist Joshua (Joshua Emeje from Igala) arrived with fifteen fine young Bassa men who had walked twenty-four miles from Meteni. Then came Evangelist Akpan (from the southern part of Nigeria working as a missionary in Bassa) with a contingent of six from the Dimbeku church.

When the service began we had a congregation of seventy-three, and as we sang the opening hymn, "There is power in the Blood", my thoughts went back ten years to the time when we first entered Bassa country. One remembered the first contacts with a suspicious people, and the bitter disappointment when a whole year passed and not a single person had responded. There was the joyful recollection of the first break. About twelve people began to drop in on the way to their farms, leaving implements outside the church door, and eventually, that never-to-be-forgotten day when four stood up and signified their willingness to follow Christ. Yes! there is power in the Blood!

After the service, five men came to ask that a teacher (preacher) be sent to their town. They live a few miles from Meteni and had come with Joshua. Reluctantly we had to explain that there was no one to send. These five, who walked twenty-six miles to ask for a teacher, typify the heart-hunger of the great mass of the Bassa people.

45

Thousands are perishing without the knowledge that God loves them. Civilisation is advancing. A government road, with cement bridges, is under construction and by the end of this year it will have opened up the whole country, bringing motor lorries and traders, many of whom will be proselytising Muslims.

The new, and as yet unused, mission house at Toto was still awaiting an occupant. Just prior to Archie MacLellan's time for leave, Christmas 1947, a new man was due in Bassa, David Gilmore. When Archie travelled to Jos for supplies Toto Mission House was burnt to the ground. Evidence pointed to a bush fire being the cause, but the circumstances were decidedly suspicious. In any event the house was never rebuilt, and the area is still virtually unevangelised.

In 1950 when David Gilmore was drawing to the end of his first tour in Bassa he wrote home from Kanyehu:

> We are still joyfully holding the fort, although very disappointed that Mr. Curry failed to pass the medical officer and relieve the Bassa garrison. A short time ago a woman professed faith in the Saviour and burnt her idols. Then she had a severe test in the matter of health, but in a few days came through to victory. She is always present at the services and showing a real change of heart. Kanyehu is still a centre of light in this land of darkness and witchcraft, and the number attending the services is very heartening. In fact we have installed some new 'pews' this week. Later it will be a new church.

A definite movement of the Holy Spirit was being felt in Bassa at this time and by the end of the year there were signs of further encouragement. Ken Williams came to Bassa with a simple plan to double the number of people hearing the Word when he was on a preaching tour. He writes:

> At each place we visited the people listened eagerly to the gospel message. In all the meetings during the fif-

teen days, about fifteen hundred people heard the Word of God. One special feature of this trek was the number of women who heard the message. It has an amusing side. Try, as we would, and tell the Chief concerned in plain English, or plain Igbirra, Hausa, or Bassa, as the case might be, to collect the women as well to hear the Word of God, we always arrived to find plenty of males, but no females. Hence we decided to adopt new tactics to bring along the fair sex. A threat that I would visit them individually to preach to them in their compounds if they did not come to the meeting produced some effect. Then we thought of a better way. When word would come from the chief that all was ready for me to speak to his people, and, on arriving and finding no women, after we had asked that they be called, I just sat down and announced to the chief that I would not commence the meeting until he had called all the women, as I had asked him to do. This had the desired effect. The poor old fellow would look at me and laugh, but, knowing I meant what I said, he would immediately send messengers to call the women, and they always responded to the call.

At one place on the Igala side of the Benue, the Igbirra and Bassa chiefs had collected about one hundred and forty of their people to hear the gospel one morning, but, as usual, all men. On asking for the women the two chiefs found it rather difficult to find an excuse for their absence, for, being morning, the usual excuse, "They are preparing the evening meal," could not be pleaded. On hearing our 'usual' — which, I must admit, we were by this time beginning to enjoy — the two chiefs had a good laugh, and went off personally to collect the Igbirra and Bassa women. In a few minutes the ladies began to appear, at first in ones and twos, then in crowds, until we had over one hundred women in the meeting. The two chiefs returned with an air of triumph evidently as pleased with the proceedings as we were ourselves. And how those women listened to the gospel message, especially the Igbirras, as through two interpreters, I told them the old, old story of God's redeeming love! Our hearts rejoice as we remember the promise: "My Word shall not return unto me void . . . but it shall accomplish . . . and prosper."

One Sunday evening after an open-air meeting a heathen man said he had been thinking for some time about the Christian and the Moslem way, and, after hearing that the Christian Way was the only Way, he said he would like to become a Christian, and asked us to pray for him. On Monday morning at Shafa a young woman came to greet me, and I had a good chat with her about the things of God. She told me that she and her friends had been watching teacher Hogan for some time to see, in effect, if he were genuine. She admitted that they had come to the conclusion that "he lived what he preached" and said she would like to follow God's way. She promised to come to the church on Sundays to hear more of the Word of God. Please remember these two in your prayers, for I believe both of them are seeking God.

The movement, which began when David Gilmore was here, of people coming saying they wish to follow God, to repent from the old way, and to burn their ju-ju and idols, goes steadily forward. The first Sunday after Mr. Gilmore went away, a young man stood up at the close of the morning service in Kanyehu and announced that he wished to repent and follow God. That same evening he publicly burned his ju-ju and said he really trusted the Lord Jesus. Mr. Efanga and I both warned him that he would be tested in his new faith. The test came sooner than we had expected. On the Monday morning he was bitten by a snake when going to his farm. We treated the bite, and again reminded him of what we had said about being tested in the Christian life. We committed him to the Lord in prayer, and, I am glad to say, he stood the test well and came through with flying colours. Prayer was answered for him and he recovered.

On Tuesday of this week an older woman from the Igala side and a young man from another place came to see me. They both said they wished to repent and to follow the Lord Jesus Christ. I was asked by the woman if I would come down to her home town on this side of the Benue, as she wished to publicly burn her ju-ju, and I could also speak to the other people in her compound. So I went down to her village some miles below Umaisha on the banks of the Benue. She brought out her ju-ju and she herself "put the fire under". This kind of thing is going on steadily in other parts of the district. The Holy Spirit seems to be dealing with them individually, and leading them to repentance and to faith in Christ.

Eileen Williams found opportunities among the Muslim women in Umaisha. The District Head gave her a guide to lead her to the right compounds where the women were kept in hiding from the rest of the community. Starting out early each morning for a week, armed with permission from the respective husbands — most of whom were pleased that their wives were receiving a visit, she generally found a warm reception. The fact that most men had their full quota of four wives, with the consequent army of small children, meant that there was a considerable gathering at each stop. Some of the wives were very withdrawn and unwilling to speak, or answer questions. Others spoke up for themselves, stating simply, "I like your word." At one place the women stayed behind a door while the preaching went on in the yard. Afterwards Eileen was able to go into the house just to greet them.

At Toto, where Islam was strongly entrenched, she gained permission to visit one of the Muslim compounds, but on arrival at the entrance was told to wait. She sat it out patiently in the scorching heat for a good fifteen minutes, and, at last, was ushered into the inner court. Here it was immediately obvious that, far from being out of impoliteness, the long wait had been to give them all time to dress up in their finest clothes in honour of this visitor.

There were three families of four wives each drawn up neatly in two rows, all wearing brightly coloured dresses and head-ties. A mass of children stood quietly by, or clung nervously to their mothers. What a wonderful opportunity this was to present the Saviour, who had laid aside His glory to come and redeem us! They gave their full attention to the message and were most insistent that a return visit would be welcomed.

One of the Muslim husbands bore the title 'Chief of Beggars'. This was the first time Mrs. Williams had realised that there was a recognised profession of beggars. He seemed to be a man of some importance, having already acquired three shut-in wives. He was currently looking for a fourth, when, as he put it, he had . . . "begged a little longer to reach the full amount of the dowry."

Nigeria was becoming very education conscious in the mid-50's. Teachers were being trained to meet the needs of hundreds of schools which were being built. Inevitably, missions became more than ever involved in this work and fine Christians were recruited to take on teaching and administration responsibilities in mission schools. One such man in Bassa was Mr. Hogan, who, with his wife came to Shafa from their home in the south. He was not only a school teacher but a true missionary as well, who, like many others, was prepared to leave home, friends, tribe and language area to take the Word of God to another 'nation'. He and his wife laboured faithfully for several years building up the schools and sending out graduates who proved to be some of the finest Christians in Bassa. Soon after Ken Williams had arrived at Kanyehu, Mr. Hogan asked him to visit Shafa to survey for a new school to take the place of a now delapidated one, and to move, with the whole village, to the edge of the motor road about two miles distant.

Although the site was obtained and duly marked out on that, the first of Ken's visits, it took a further three years for official permission to be granted. Ken Williams and David Gilmore wanted the people of Shafa to put their own effort into the project, so, to encourage them, the two missionaries decided to work on the job with them — David on the block laying, Ken on the joinery. However, before they could begin, David was transferred to Igala, leaving Ken alone. He describes the way the job was completed and some of the frustration along the way:

The building was to be sixty feet long and twenty feet wide with two large classrooms and a store in the middle. It was not without a feeling of trepidation that I began, before a crowd of spectators, to level the foundation and lay the first row of blocks. Of mason's labourers there was no shortage; all the schoolboys were there and quite a number of young men of the village. Everybody was eager to help and soon I was almost fenced in by piles of well-mixed mud (or mortar) and neatly-made sand blocks.

After watching for some time, Teacher Hogan suggested he would try, and I started him on one of the end walls. Then Dan, my cook, thought he had got the idea and he started on the other end. One by one the number of builders increased until it was difficult to find space for everybody. There was many a squabble, for all wanted to build rather than fetch mud from the pit and blocks from the pile, but once law and order were established the work proceeded apace.

Incidentally, this united effort revealed the tremendous influence exerted by Teacher Hogan, not only amongst the schoolboys, but also the older folk — pagans, Moslems, and Christians — he is highly respected by all.

By 20th February we were ready for the doors and windows and I returned to Kanyehu. Then came our first big disappointment: the sawyer had promised to have the timber ready, but it was 24th March before the first consignment arrived. Less than a month to go before the rains! How we prayed and worked! Here it should be mentioned that they were Igbirras who walked seven miles to Ugya to pick up the timber, carried it eleven miles to Kanyehu, and then bore the completed door and window frames another eighteen miles to Shafa. All this, as well as the building, was done voluntarily. Such a thing had never been known in this area and it was most encouraging.

I worked on the joinery almost day and night and by 1st April was ready to return to Shafa. The builders rallied round again. It was a battle against time. Heavy rains had already fallen and many half-finished houses collapsed. But our walls — sheltered by constant prayer — stood the test. Then the timber for the roof arrived, and by 22nd April we were ready to hand over to the thatchers. Dan and I returned to Kanyehu, somewhat weary, but rejoicing that our building would be ready for the wet season, though much inside work remained to be done.

The Shafa people are rightly proud of their new school, in the construction of which they had such a vital share. It has been valued at £150 and the only cash outlay was £25 for timber, which the people themselves contributed.

We look beyond the actual building, however, and feel that this is a place where young lives will not only come under Christian influence, but into personal contact with the Lord Jesus Christ. We have planted, it may be left to others to do the watering, and we believe that God will give a mighty increase. Eternity alone will reveal the part the school has played and will play in spreading the Gospel Light in this dark, dark area.

Praise God for Teacher Hogan and his wife, products of our Qua Iboe Church, who have been in a very real sense 'foreign' missionaries in lonely Shafa.

Besides such monumental practical work, Ken Williams spent a great deal of his time, with the help of several Nigerians, working on translations: a revised and enlarged hymn book, a Bassa "Way of Salvation", and some of the Scriptures. His major accomplishment was yet to be, however. After he had officially retired from the work in Nigeria, mainly due to Eileen's ill health, he returned alone, at great sacrifice to himself and his wife, to complete the translation of the Bassa New Testament. With Paul Imoh, Simon Asada and Noah, from Igala, this invaluable work was carried to completion and presented to the Bible Society for publication.

Many there are who gave themselves wholeheartedly to work in establishing the Kingdom of

God in Bassa. Most of these will remain unmentioned here, and some are not known, except to God. Others are part of the rich vein of faithfulness traced in the rock of testing.

Such was David Ocholi from Igala, a humble, quiet, reliable man who left all to follow the Master to foreign parts and there proclaim that "Jesus saves". His schooling was minimal but, taught of the Spirit, he would preach with a depth of understanding of the Truth worthy of the 'great' pulpits of the western world. Joshua Emeje, and his brother Jonah, also from Igala, were of like calibre to David Ocholi, continuing for years in Bassa before returning to serve among the Igalas all the rest of their lives.

A steady stream of men and women from the south made the five-hundred-mile journey to Bassa to share their faith with a people of so distinctly different culture. And, as the church grew, there were the many fine Christians of the Bassa, Igbirra and other tribes who lived out the gospel among their own people.

Daniel Turkura, one of Mr. Hogan's prime pupils was sent on to Idah by David Gilmore to be under Herbert Dickson's fatherly care whilst he concluded his primary education. He later became the head-master at Dimbeku, sometimes working for months without a salary. He led the triumphant procession of his pupils all the way to Oguma for the launching ceremony of John's Gospel on its arrival in Bassa.

Mr. Dickson was later to write of his final meeting with Daniel:

> When staying overnight with Mr. and Mrs. Hyslop, missionaries working independently in Bassa, my host asked, "Did you not bring up Daniel Turkura?" When I replied, "Yes," he went on to tell me of his academic brilliance and that he is now Assistant Registrar at Jos Uni-

53

versity. Mr. Hyslop could not have spoken more highly of this man, who has been helping him in many ways with the Bassa language. I was delighted to hear this but still had no hope of meeting Daniel as Jos could not be fitted into my itinerary.

The Lord has wonderful surprises in store for His children! The very next day, travelling with David Griffiths along a very rough bit of bush road on the way to Sardauna, suddenly a small lorry appeared, coming in the opposite direction. As the road was so narrow both vehicles had to stop and negotiate carefully to pass unscathed. Mr. Griffiths recognised someone in the lorry and began talking to him. Then he spotted another and cried out, "Daniel Turkura, where have you come from? Do you see who is with me? Mr. Dickson!"

Before I had time to take in what was happening, there was Daniel at my side, exploding with delight. I need not describe the joy of that brief interview. Suddenly Daniel ran to his transport and as suddenly returned.

"Baba," he said, "I have nothing to give you, but take this to buy something for yourself." He handed me five Naira, equivalent to over three pounds in British currency.

What a thrilling encounter! Who but the Lord could have arranged for Daniel, employed in far away Jos, to meet me in the heart of Bassa bush? Who else could give us the joy of looking into each other's faces once more, and having that brief moment of fellowship together?

Amodu, that master of many languages, whose full name is Amodu David Ossabo, was a staunch Moslem when he first heard the gospel as he interpreted for Herbert Dickson. It took some weeks, and a great deal of earnest enquiry on his part, before he came to know Jesus as his Saviour. Once that fellowship was established, Amodu launched himself into the work of God with a willing heart. There can be no doubt that he was a key, prepared by the Lord, to unlock the complicated languages of the Bassa area for the emissaries of the gospel. His education over the years included Okene and Gindiri Teachers' Colleges, the Qua Iboe Bible College at Abak and a course of training in the United Kingdom for supervision of Boys' Brigade work in Nigeria.

These and many others worked alongside the missionaries already mentioned and those who followed them. Michael and Margaret Kelsey were in Bassa when Gwen Gold first came to Nigeria. For Gwen this was a particular joy, for Margaret, née Woodward, had been the very one, used of God, to lead her to the Lord. Gwen happily visited her friends in Kanyehu but her first response to Bassa was characteristically blunt: "I could never work in this place." Perhaps the Lord smiled at this — He had other plans.

David Griffiths, joined later by his wife Léon, took up the reins of the work in 1960 and, with commendable fortitude and against a background of many disappointments, carried on longer than any of their predecessors. So when the Lord re-commissioned Gwen and sent her first to Bassa she was to be welcomed and initiated there by David and Léon.

CHAPTER 5

Burning Heat

For David and Léon Griffiths the work at Kanyehu required infinite patience. How wonderfully God suits His workers to the task. This couple was just right for the years when those with less endurance would have given up. These two persevered in travelling and teaching among the believers whose spiritual growth seemed to have slowed to a snail's pace. There were many crushing disappointments as brother bickered with brother, and several turned aside from the way completely. Through it all the Lord endued David and Léon with a supernatural optimism. Their joy knew no bounds when they saw the Holy Spirit at work, even in the smallest matter.

At Kakana there was probably not one Christian among the few who gathered in the grass-roofed shelter to hear David preach, but they listened intently and later begged for a man to be sent to teach them the truths of God. Jonathan, a Bassa Christian, went to live among them. Within a year they had built a mud-walled church and several had found faith in Christ. Such was their zeal that they offered their village for the next annual conference for the whole area. This would entail accommodating and feeding, at their own expense, all the visitors. Léon wrote about this conference:

> Come with us to Kakana, a small village eleven miles from Kanyehu. One hundred and thirty-five people from twenty-seven villages have gathered to hear the Word of God. Some have walked many miles, they have crossed streams, one man has cycled from a place thirty-five miles away and here they are squatting on crude seats and rush mats waiting for the meeting to begin.
>
> A young African announces a hymn, another prays, yet another speaks and the conference has really begun. Every meeting is similar with various ones taking part, especially two Bible School students on vacation. On Sunday morning there is a note of triumph as we all head for the stream where five men and one woman are to be baptised. Next follows the Lord's Supper with the believers participating . . . We all felt this was a most worthwhile Conference.

These annual gatherings of Christians from a wide area were times of joy and fellowship for all, not least the missionaries themselves. Their value lay in mutual encouragement and in the hearing of deeper truths than they might in their isolated churches. Léon used to compare them to mini Keswicks — though the imagination would have to stretch almost as far as from Keswick to Kanyehu to make the connection. Sitting on logs perched precariously on forked sticks, shaded from the merciless sun by the branches of a mango tree, or, in the evening, wrapped from head to foot in the 'night cloth' against the ravages of the voracious mosquito, there was little resemblance to meetings in the 'big tent'.

But, crossing many language barriers was the same idea: 'All one in Christ Jesus'. And the messages, adapted to an African's environment, were exactly the same: 'Walking in the Spirit,' 'Tithing,' 'Christ's coming as prophesied in the Old Testament,' 'His Passion,' and such like matters of primary importance to all Christians. And after the conference the same great question begs an answer: how much of the precious seed will bear fruit?

By the end of 1966 David and Léon were convinced that an adequate medical work based at Kanyehu was a priority. How often were they distressed at illness, accident, or death around them with only rudimentary medical care available to relieve the suffering. They, for their part, did what they could; but an insight into how formidable a task this was for non-medics is given by Léon:

> We kept some medicines at the mission house in those days and every day, after breakfast, our first job was to deal with the few patients who had gathered on the side verandah. We had a simple chart with symptoms and drugs which were appropriate — this basic information given to David by Robert Thompson was now augmented by some medical books which I had brought out with me. David used to pull the occasional tooth and there were always ulcers to be dressed. The fellow who used to interpret for us would ask the usual questions while we waited anxiously for the "case history" and tried to reach a diagnosis or at least match up the symptoms with our chart. It is amazing how often the treatment did seem to be effective in spite of our ignorance, but it was almost frightening to see the trust these poor folk placed in us. Of course, they had nowhere else to go apart from their native doctors.

From the point of view of Christian compassion only, this situation clamoured for attention, but, from experience in many other centres in Nigeria, it was also clear that such a work would open many a heart to the gospel. Léon wrote home:

> A great wailing broke out among the people as the two men carried the lifeless body of the woman into the compound, between the round mud houses with their overhanging grass roofs. They no longer carried her with care but almost ran in their eagerness to deposit their

grim burden. Seconds before she had been lifted from the car barely alive after we abandoned a desperate attempt to get medical aid, made in answer to the relative's fervent pleas. Another soul had passed into eternity. Had she responded to the gospel that she heard preached in those days of agonising pain? Could she understand? These are questions we cannot answer but we can continue telling out the Good News of salvation to the living. Unrelieved, utter despair had descended like a dark cloud on that compound. Women, beating the air with their arms, wailed in rising frenzy while the men shook with sobs.

Nearly a mile away on our compound Josiah paused to hear the familiar sounds which always denote a pagan death. A Bassa woman came forward to squeeze our hands in greeting as we walked away. Some understanding, some sympathy passed between us in that moment, which broke through the barriers of tribe and did not require a spoken language to express. It was a "Thank you," mingled with a plea for help. Can we tell them of a Saviour's love and not have compassion when we see them sick and dying? The answer is an emphatic "No" — yet are we responding adequately to this need? "Why is it that the Mission is so short of doctors?" asks a local Christian, when we try to explain why only one short visit by a nurse for general clinics has been possible in over two years. What can we say?

Imagine the joy the Griffiths, and the Bassa people experienced when they learned that Gwen Gold was on the way to Kanyehu to open up a medical work there. As she covered the distance from Liverpool to Lagos and on to Kanyehu, Gwen had time to reflect on the great privilege which was hers in having a second opportunity to serve the Lord in Nigeria. The old natural fears were there again as on her first tour, with the added concern over the special difficulties of Bassa, not least her isolation from other medical advice or help.

She wondered too how she and the Griffiths would get on. David and Léon had the same fears. They were so totally different, and so used to working alone in their own particular way. Gwen was bustlingly urgent about her work, David and Léon were quietly methodical. Would they be able to work together? As the distance in miles between them narrowed, they came to the same conclusion: for the sake of the Lord and His work they would do their utmost to 'accept' each other. As it happened, they all discovered, to their delight, a warm friendship, and the atmosphere at Kanyehu was one of a loving family.

Gwen's arrival in Bassa was a case of 'being thrown in at the deep end' and the water was hot! There are two kinds of weather at Kanyehu, oven hot and sauna hot. Take your pick and you will immediately wish that you had not. As the full force of the May heat poured upon Gwen, sucking away like a vampire at her reserve of energy, she wondered again how she could do a full day's work in a place where sitting still was enough to produce rivers of perspiration.

Before she could properly unpack, a baby was presented to her by a distraught family. The mother had bled to death. There was no one to care for the infant. Could the new 'Sister' help? Gwen took a deep breath, looked up to her Father and said,, "Yes." And so little Nuhu became the first of many babies she 'adopted'.

On the third day the Emir of Nasarawa and other V.I.P.s came to view the site for the new dispensary. Discussions were very cordial and the promise of government support for the project was given there and then. Everyone knew that from the smiles and nods of approval to the opening of the new dispensary building would be a while! In the meantime one of the most basic requirements was shelter for the waiting patients. It was disheartening to find how much persuasion it took to get a few sticks erected, and some bundles of grass on top to provide a bit of thatch. Gwen learned quickly that such was often the village response though the request be made for its benefit. Yet she settled down to her work in these most primitive of conditions with the knowledge that, sometime in the future, she would have her dispensary. As far as the patients were concerned they had no intention of waiting; as long as there was help and care available, the surroundings were of no significance. After all, the nearest alternative medical help was one hundred and ten miles away.

Of course Sister Gold was expected to cope with every emergency. Accidents and complications, such as would send modern hospitals into full alert, were presented to her with wide-eyed expectation that she would snatch the dying from the gates of death. At times the lather of perspiration which broke out on her had little to do with the heat of the day, but rather dismay at the enormity of her responsibility as she examined the desperately ill.

Certainly she prayed. From the very beginning she prayed; but it was only gradually that prayer began to replace panic with a quiet confidence in her Lord. She would not always succeed, but she could always pray — for herself, for the sick and with the relatives. David and Léon were called into this ministry with her whenever it was possible. It became a common thing for specific prayer to be made for recovery of those whose only real hope lay in the direct intervention of God. Many healings were effected in such a manner as to be truly miraculous, and at other times special wisdom was given regarding treatment in the absence of proper diagnostic information.

A young lad was brought to Gwen with advanced tetanus. She examined him thoughtfully. The state of the boy was pathetic and his wild eyes revealed the paralysing dread within. Relatives standing hopefully nearby could have no idea how close to death he was, nor how little even modern medicines could help. Gwen confided in the Griffiths that this case looked hopeless. To ease the horror of the disease, however, she kept the boy heavily sedated, while prayer was made for him and his people.

After many days when the youngster should have died, there was a very slight change in his condition. Slowly, so slowly, he improved under care and in answer to prayer — till one day Gwen came upon him in the compound taking mangoes. For once she was not displeased at having her fruit stolen.

A woman came in with a slice cut out of her scalp. She had been carrying her heavy water pot when it broke over her head. Gwen wanted to know where the missing piece was. Those around looked at her in amazement. Whatever would she want that for? A search party went back to the scene of the accident, the piece was found and borne to the dispensary in an old cigarette packet. Gwen went to work with her suturing skills till the errant section was back where it belonged. It healed perfectly.

Gwen was rarely ill. True, in her early days in Igala she had to be taken to Ochadamu Medical Centre on several occasions, suffering from exhaustion and one or other of the common ailments. Dr. Bill Holley finally insisted on her having adequate convalescence and after that she was much better in health. But in later years she did not even take prophylactics. On one occasion though, soon after her arrival in Kanyehu, she had a severe bout of malaria. There was great concern as her temperature remained at 104°F, untouched by any of the anti-malarial drugs. Léon was on virtual sentry duty outside the house to turn away the patients, explaining that 'Sister' was more ill than they. Just as she was turning back yet another family, Léon noticed a bundle of dirty cloth. She pulled the cloth aside and found that she was staring at the badly scalded face of a baby. She was so taken aback that she exclaimed, "Oh, it's a baby!" Gwen staggered out of bed and came to see.

Soon the little mite was on the dispensary table, and the awful extent of the scalding was apparent — only the feet and ankles had escaped.

"What happened?" Gwen asked.

"The baby pulled a pot of boiling water over himself," replied the distraught parents.

It looked as if the child had actually fallen into the pot head first. Gwen turned away and spoke to Léon in English: "There is no hope, but for the mother's sake we must do something." She gathered some dressings and began preparing an injection, but even as she drew it up, the baby died.

Léon was wholly unable to speak, but Gwen began talking quietly with those parents: begging the husband not to blame the wife, and assuring the distraught mother that God loved her child and that he was now safe with Him. She went on to witness with great sympathy and understanding to that Moslem family, completely ignoring her own physical discomfort.

Then there was the demonic. In such a place, never far below the surface, is the involvement with the occult. In the first month Gwen noted the heavy emphasis her patients laid on wearing protective charms. They rarely saw any disparity between consulting both the witch doctor and the Christian Sister. After all, why not cover every angle? Sometimes the patient would show more

definite signs of satanic interference, as Gwen
described in her first prayer letter from Kanyehu:

> This last weekend brought forth a ding-dong battle with
> the spirit priest and the witch doctor. A girl was brought
> to me screaming the place down that 'they' were beating
> her. Her husband assured me that the devil had caught
> her! On to the scene came the ju-ju priest, ranting and
> raving, blaming the husband for allowing the girl to
> "hear the Word of God." After a bit he stormed off, still
> shouting in a fury. I gave the girl a sedative, prayed with
> them and they left all calm and peaceful.
>
> In the evening I cycled to the far end of the village and
> there found Juma in a pathetic state: lying on a mat
> under a grass shelter, scarcely any clothing on her and
> surrounded by a bodyguard of women. As I walked up to
> her she began shrieking like a dervish — 'the demons
> were beating her' — and flung herself into mid air, only
> to be caught and held down by the women.
>
> The priest then stood up and went on at great length.
> Musa, our Evangelist, would not tell me all he said, so I
> gather that it was hardly complimentary to me! I talked
> with her father, but he assured me that his father had
> lived worshipping the devil and had died in the devil, he
> would also die in the devil and likewise his child. The
> witch doctor chimed in and said that this sickness could
> not be cured by white people's medicine. I agreed, and
> added that it would not be cured by his medicine either,
> for she was obviously worse. Only God could do anything
> for her; can the devil drive out the devil?
>
> David and Léon and I met for prayer that evening and
> Juma was much in our thoughts. We should not have
> been surprised, therefore, when Musa came to say that
> her father had suddenly relented and allowed the girl to
> come to stay on the mission compound with the district
> evangelist (himself a converted ju-ju man) and his wife.
> Juma is still a very sick girl but there have been no
> further attacks since she left her father's compound.

This incident, and many like it, brought home
more fully to the missionaries and the local believers that they were engaged in a supernatural battle, that the fight would be fierce, and that the only
weapons suitable were spiritual, not human. They

all needed to learn to use these weapons, and quickly.

On Sunday evenings the missionary trio loved to sing together in the house. They sang often from the "Pilgrimage and Conflict" section of the hymnbooks: "Stand up, stand up for Jesus"; "Who is on the Lord's side?" and "Christian, dost thou see them, on the Holy ground, How the powers of darkness compass thee around?" They were indeed keenly aware of those powers.

Apart from all the heat and pressure already mentioned, there was another problem boiling up around them. At first the very remoteness of their sphere of activity seemed to be a sure buffer against the political storm which was rising in Nigeria, and politics, of course, was something in which they were wholly uninvolved. But the disturbing winds were too strong to leave Kanyehu unaffected. The true horror of tribal hatred and mistrust hit them full in the face one day and put all their lives in great danger.

Japheth had helped Gwen in the house when she had been in Ugwolawo and Ibaji, his home area. On her return to Nigeria he had gladly followed her to Bassa despite the great cultural and language differences. But the tragedy of civil war was tearing at the heart of the nation, and old animosities were erupting into ugly incidents everywhere. Japheth was in Umaisha, five miles from Kanyehu, when he was stopped and questioned by a policeman.

Where was his tax certificate? Japheth did not have it with him. Who was he? Was he not a 'foreigner' since he had no tribal markings common to this area? Japheth explained who he was, that he worked for Miss Gwen Gold at Kanyehu and that he was from the Igala tribe, thus a northener like everyone else here. He was not believed and was dragged off followed by a swelling hostile crowd.

When the news reached Gwen she was not too disturbed. Surely all that was needed was a trip to Umaisha, a simple explanation, and the whole thing would be cleared up with a friendly handshake. David, Léon and Gwen set off in the little Volkswagon Beetle. To their surprise, and considerable shock, however, their story was not believed. Instead they found themselves at the centre of an angry bloodthirsty mob.

"Kill him! Kill him! Kill him!" they chanted, pressing frighteningly close to Japheth and the missionaries.

A policeman pushed forward and roughly grabbed the seventeen-year-old lad.

"No!" screamed Gwen, "He is my son."

With this she threw her arms around Japheth, and Léon did the same, so that he was cocooned in their embrace against the danger.

For what seemed like an eternity, the furious pack faced the two women. It would have taken just one blow from any of the powerful men around them to have sent them sprawling and set a pattern of violence which would have ended in certain death for Japheth if not for his protectors. Gwen and Léon, their hearts pounding, resolutely stared back at the would-be executioners. Everything in their stance proclaimed, "To kill this boy, you must kill us first."

Léon Griffiths takes up the story:

> It seemed almost inevitable that the boy would be torn to pieces before our eyes. We had to walk through that mob to the charge office and the Lord wonderfully undertook as we flanked the lad, our arms around him, and David pressed in at the rear. We never could fathom what happend to that crowd. Suddenly we were no longer aware of

them. The Lord held them back like the Red Sea for the Israelites.

Later that night we were allowed to take the boy home with us, but rumours had preceded us, and when we arrived we were met by some of our people, coming forward weeping, believing Japheth had been killed. Their tears turned to joy when they saw him alive. We were so impressed by the love displayed by these folk — in sharp contrast to the hate witnessed shortly before.

Some trying days followed as we had to go to Divisional H.Q. with a police escort, but the Emir finally contacted the District Officer at Keffi. The Lord undertook in marvellous ways and at last his identity was accepted.

After this it was deemed best to send Japheth back to his own people. With great regret Gwen took him out of the danger zone and sent him on his way. She would miss his cheerful company and his faithfulness in all his duties. He had not merely been a houseboy. His support for Gwen had included caring for orphaned babies whilst she was away on treks, watching over the security of the buildings and going to great lengths to see that she had variety in her diet. He would be hard to replace.

Japheth spent some weeks in Ibaji but he was not happy. His reasoning of the situation went something like this:

"What am I doing here when it is obvious that the Lord wants me in Kanyehu serving Him, and Sister Gold? If the Lord delivered me from danger last time, why should I run away and not trust Him to do it again? Anyway, if I am killed, it is better to die doing what God wants of me than to live outside His will."

To Gwen's great delight and encouragement Japheth returned to Kanyehu.

Still waiting for the dispensary to be built, and working and living under very primitive conditions, Gwen sought to meet the medical needs of growing numbers of people. The work at Kanyehu alone would have been ample for one nurse, but she was aware of other areas where a regular weekly clinic would be so much appreciated. Just to contemplate how much effort would be required to take a day or two each week away from the base was a daunting prospect. David and Léon offered their help, with the idea that they could also use the trips in conjunction with their own preaching and visiting ministry. So, with earnest prayer, they all took a deep breath and launched out yet further.

Despite import restrictions an estate car was provided, and they set off eventually to hold the first of the regular clinics at Shafan Abakwa. The drums must have sounded far and wide for, to Gwen's amazement, and not a little horror, one hundred and fifteen patients turned up that day! Some, no doubt, came because they did not want to miss the excitement; others because the clinic being only once a week meant they needed to anticipate the illness they might have in the next seven days.

The new car was a boon, but it had its restrictions. There were places only accessible by river transport. David and Léon describe a journey to one such place where another regular clinic was envisaged:

In England it was the day of the Boat Race and we imagined the two crews straining every muscle to gain a few inches, the flotilla of small craft following at a distance and the excited crowds lining the banks of the Thames. Far away in Nigeria a little canoe was being propelled furiously up the River Benue. Was the lone poler less earnest than the Oxford and Cambridge blues in his efforts to reach the goal? Wasn't this the chance for which he had waited, to bring medical help to his village? Had he not stood a few months before at the graveside of his sister, who might have been saved had help been nearer? His face was glowing, his strong muscles were rippling and his dark skin glistened with perspiration as the unrelenting sun beat down. After two hours we came near his village and stepped out into the shallow water where a crowd of noisy children were swimming and splashing towards us. Soon they encircled our canoe, all trying to hold our hands at once, while someone guided the little craft between the sandbanks.

Once ashore we were taken to the church building where the local Christians told Gwen Gold, our nursing sister, that they would like a regular clinic and that this building could be used. Then we went to visit the village chief, who assured us of his support and promised to provide canoe and paddlers to transport the nurse and her helpers with medicines. Please pray for this new venture. There is no motor road to this village and the nearest hospital that side of the river is two days' journey away.

Some time later, when this clinic at Ozugbe was well established, Gwen was regularly faced with attending two hundred patients in the steaming heat and noise of the tiny church building. And this was squeezed between two long, tiring canoe journeys, loading and unloading of medicines and a double trip by car to and from the river.

With all these more obvious pressures there was another about which few people knew. Gwen had injured her back and was in almost constant pain. She wore a brace at times to take some of the strain, but, as can be easily imagined, this device had its own form of torture in a climate of such relentless heat.

As the medical work expanded, and with the prospect of doubling the land area at Kanyehu to include the new dispensary and the sister's house, so also the number of people hearing the gospel every day greatly increased. At times nine languages might be needed in a single day to communicate with so cosmopolitan a group as gathered at the clinics. It is impossible to judge the extent of the witness for Christ flowing out from Kanyehu in a babble of tongues to so vast and diverse a people. The depth of penetration of the message to any given individual would be even more difficult to gauge, since contact might be broken entirely after the completion of treatment, and the patient would return to his pagan, or Moslem home. Many were the prayers which followed these folk, like soft showers to water the tender seed of truth.

It must not be thought that Gwen sailed through all adversity, pain, loneliness and a punishing work load without, at times, sinking into despair. Particularly after David and Léon went on leave, the isolation of Kanyehu and the slow progress of the life of the church began to take its toll. She reached rock bottom several times and was almost ready to give up before the end of her first tour. She learned more about her inner dross than she ever imagined possible. When her temper flared, or her compassion failed, she would contemplate her weaknesses with sorrow. But the Lord's compassion towards her never failed. She would be picked up by His loving arms, and, through a scripture, a tape, a song, would be nursed back to the place of contentment and joy in Him. She did not yet know that her Lord was beginning to draw for her such a deep draught of blessing as would bring her refreshment enough to touch all her longing for joyous living, even in Bassa.

CHAPTER 6

Stampede

When Gwen returned to Nigeria after leave she did not go immediately to Kanyehu but spent five months in the Sudan Interior Mission Language School, Kano. This proved to be so worthwhile that other workers in Bassa were later to follow her lead. As Gwen began to use Hausa more fluently in the following months, she enjoyed new liberty in communicating directly. Of course, there was still the problem of so many other language groups, many unfamiliar with Hausa, so that interpreters were still needed.

Noah, a Bassa man, had completed four years of Bible training at Karu and was by this time assisting with the work at Kanyehu. He offered to help Gwen develop her use of Hausa by giving her instruction two hours a week. When some small payment was tended for this service he was quite indignant — why should he be paid to help his friend share the gospel more freely with his people? This lovely attitude gave Gwen no small delight.

The mission house, in use while Gwen waited for her more permanent dwelling, was old but pleasantly constructed with large rooms and high ceilings to give maximum air circulation. The verandah was hardly ever free of visitors, patients, or orphans being brought four times a day for their feeds. All the activity, the constant demands of the needy, the weak, the disturbed, filled up Gwen's days, and sometimes nights as well, to capacity. When she felt overburdened with work and interruptions she would remind herself that it was best to be busy, otherwise her loneliness would overwhelm her.

She had quite a 'family'. Nuhu was now three years of age, tubby and somewhat bandy-legged. He tottered about all over the house and compound, chattering away in Bassa, or English, and usually closely followed by one or other of Gwen's dogs. Daji was a child Gwen had inherited from the Griffiths when they went on leave. Of the four others, three required bottle feeding. The smallest rejoiced in the name of Nyezhogembi. A big name for such a small scrap of two months old. The name means 'the world is a hard place'. Indeed it was so for him, and several times he tried to slip out of it.

Abibetu was the one little girl Gwen was 'mothering' and, to use her own expression, "a real poppet". She was eight months old when Gwen wrote home about her at the end of 1970:

> A happier, prettier, more contented wee girl would be hard to find. She comes from a Moslem background but her foster mother has attended one of the services and loves to hear the gospel records. She is such a nice person, so quiet and with a natural grace.

It was only just over a month later when Gwen wrote again:

> Abibetu, the beautiful little girl of whom I told you in my last letter, died while I was in Jos in December. She had never been sick before — it could have been cerebral malaria. We had all come to love her so much. Her foster mother has never had children of her own and had

poured out all her love on this wee mite. Her grief would have been easier to see had she wept and shrieked and torn her clothes, but she just stood looking so sad, with tears streaming down her cheeks.

We have two more babies since then. Another little girl under four pounds, who was having tube feeds for a while, and a wee boy. These babies make a lot of work but give so much joy that I find them a great means of relaxation.

There has been an outbreak of cholera in the area causing many deaths. One victim was Mama Daji, leaving wee Daji motherless for the second time in his life.

In order not to remove the children from their own culture, a foster mother was sought to bring up the child in her own home, while provision of feeds and health care Gwen catered for herself. Her home church helped in this project with gifts of money and clothes. Naturally a great bond grew up between Gwen and her 'children' but she was wise enough not to spoil them and make life for them and their 'mothers' intolerable. This experiment in compassion, undertaken by many missionaries in developing countries, has not always been successful, but the alternatives are even less acceptable: leaving babies to die. Gwen loved her babies, and worked so hard to save them, yet it is sad that, so far as is known, there has been no spiritual fruit from this labour.

A small Bible school had been set up at Kanyehu with eleven students. Noah was leading this work and his wife, Grace, was helping him. Gwen was delighted with the way Noah had matured, making up in part for the great disappointment over Musa. Musa had completed the same Bible course as Noah and they had graduated together. His early promise, however, was spoiled when he stubbornly refused advice and took a second wife. For

Gwen this was an unhappy period because Musa seemed unrepentant, and, in fact, later added a third wife to his family.

Even as Gwen delighted in the zeal and loyalty of Noah and Grace she had also an uneasy spirit about them, writing home:

> I would ask your prayers for this young couple. It may be wrong but we get almost afraid when we have young people of such promise, for it would seem that they are made the subject of real satanic attacks.

Unhappily her fear proved all too prophetic, for Noah left his work and his wife and went with a young student from the Bible school. Eventually Grace was reunited with her husband but the damage done to the Lord's work was great. In later years Gwen met Noah often in Jos. She found an enigma in this young man, who still spoke warmly of matters spiritual, even professed to a close personal fellowship with the Lord, yet was wholly unwilling to repent of his obvious sin.

As consolation for Gwen there was an older man, Jonathan, an evangelist at Kanyehu, whose steadfastness to the Lord was a great encouragement. Looking thinner, greyer and frailer as the years passed, he nevertheless simply bubbled over with joy. Just to be with him was a spiritual uplift. It was amazing too, Gwen found, when asking people how they came to know the Lord, how many times Jonathan's name was mentioned.

Sometimes, in doing a difficult work for the Lord, there comes along a person whose response to the missionary and the message are such as to make all the struggle so obviously worthwhile. Such a one was John Okpanachi, an Igala. He had worked with Gwen there. John was Gwen's spiritual son. Whether she had led him to the Lord is not certain, but that she nurtured him in the life of Christ is beyond doubt, and between them was a strong spiritual bond. John had advanced his education and training and was now a medical worker in the north. Whenever he could he visited Gwen in Bassa, and so shared the love of Christ with her, and her burden for the work, as to bring her delightful refreshing. When, at last, it was time to leave, John would always suggest that they have a time of prayer. A veritable oasis in a desert land.

At the beginning of 1971, Eric and Margaret Kerr came to Kanyehu to build Gwen's new home. Eric, with eight workers from Igala, worked furiously through the whole month of January to complete the house before Lily Brannan would arrive to be Gwen's new co-worker. Despite problems in obtaining cement — the civil war was over, but there were still acute shortages — the house was completed in record time and Gwen moved in. It was quite a small bungalow but might well have been a mansion for the gratitude she showed.

It was to Gwen's metal that Lily would owe her nickname. She became known as Asurfa which is Hausa for 'silver' — Gwen being Zinariya, the word for 'gold'.

Lily looked over the dry, barren scene at Kanyehu, and her thoughts went to Ezekiel 37: the valley of dry bones — "Son of Man can these bones live?" She had arrived in the dry season when Bassa looks not unlike a desert. When the rains came a remarkable and rapid transformation took place. Almost as one watched, so the green shoots and leaves appeared. The whole place took on an entirely different aspect. To Lily it spoke of the promise of life yet to burst forth in all its splendour in the Bassa church.

Lily had good cause to be optimistic, for her coming to Kanyehu was an answer to many prayers.

She had served in the south until evacuated due to the civil war. When she applied for her visa to return to Nigeria it was refused. Steadfastly she stated to the Qua Iboe Mission Home Council that the Lord had given her a promise: "Behold I set before you an open door and no man can shut it." This she believed — so not even the Nigerian Immigration Authority could change that.

Another application was made and again it was refused. By now most people were ready to give up praying, and accept the 'inevitable'. Lily stuck to her point. To their great credit, the Home Council sent in yet another application, and it was returned stamped, 'Granted'. For Lily and Gwen, as well as the rest of the mission staff, this was a sign of God's good intentions still for Bassa. "Can these dry bones live? O Lord God thou knowest."

Gwen had two dogs at this time; Snoopy and Alexia. Between them they could create quite a fierce row if anyone unwelcome came. There had been little sleep for at least a week, whilst the 'rainmakers' had rushed drumming and shrieking up and down the village day and night. Now they were on their way past the mission house for the umpteenth time leaping and screaming — to the accompaniment of the agitated hounds. The missionary's nerves were becoming almost as frayed as the dogs. She felt like barking too!

Back in the village centre the rainmakers swept into the compound of an elderly Christian called Joshua and proceeded to cut down his pawpaw tree. When Joshua attempted to stop them he was not only severely beaten but bitten too! It should be remembered that Bassas file their teeth to points, so that the bite was a serious wound. Gwen took up the poor man's cause with the chief and received some assurances that the rainmakers would be checked from such excesses.

On another occasion, when the rainmakers had been pleading with the spirits for many days causing chaos to the life of the village and medical work, Gwen was given a holy boldness to announce to the chief and the spirit priests. "You may shout and dance and sacrifice all you wish, but you will not have rain till you come to the church and beg us to pray for it."

Some of the spirit men jeered at her, others muttered curses, and still others stated that the rain would come soon. Indeed, since it was the beginning of the rainy season, there was every cause to expect them to be right.

Kanyehu, like Carmel, is on high ground with a good view to the distant hills. All around the thunder rolled and the black clouds emptied their life-giving contents on the neighbouring areas, but Kanyehu remained wholly untouched. When the situation became so desperate that there was fear of losing the season's crops, the rainmakers appeared at the church door, "Would the Christians please pray for rain?"

"Now that you know that your juju is powerless," they were told, "we will show you that our God is Lord over all. We will pray to Him for rain."

The rainmakers went off to wait, and the Christians joined in prayer. As the service finished the rain could be heard pattering on the grass roof and by the time they reached their homes the heavens had opened and Kanyehu was all but flooded.

Gwen did not always don the prophet's mantle in dealing with the rainmakers. One time she resorted to a touch of modern technology, spiced with humour. Léon describes the scene:

> There was a lad on the compound with tetanus and he was to be kept quiet. It was at the time of year when the rainmakers were out in force. They used to make a terrible row when they passed by the mission compound with their drums and bullroarers in addition to their screaming and shouting. I think we had already made some effort to stop them coming near, explaining about the sick boy. One night we heard them approaching so Gwen and I went out to the front and hid. I had an inflated paper bag and Gwen had her flashgun — when they were right near we managed a flash and bang simultaneously which sent them flying off down the hill. We must have given them the fright of their lives and I do not think they came that way again with their rainmaking procession — not as far as I remember, anyway.

Because of the epidemic of cholera the 'spirit men' were more active than anyone could remember. Gwen was resting one Saturday afternoon when she heard them coming from the direction of Umaisha. There had been such a host of these processions of late that she had no intention of getting up to see, or to quieten the dogs. However, the pace of this group seemed to be so excessively slow that she wondered if there might be something worth photographing for the record. She got up and went outside. Gwen tells the story:

> There was a poor old, old woman burdened down by a sort of heavy yoke across her neck. A juju man was walking behind her and each time she swayed or looked about to fall, he lashed her back with a bamboo — her back was streaked with blood and she had obviously fallen several times. I don't know when I've felt so 'full' over anything.
>
> At first I thought there was nothing I could do, and just said, in English, "You evil, evil men!" They just grinned, and I added in Hausa, "God will give you what you deserve for this." They grinned again and lashed out as the poor old thing took two steps forward and one backwards, just swaying and almost falling. I went out to her and put my arm around her just to give her some

support, and I thought they would not lash out at her with me near, for they do have a healthy respect for me.

She looked at me with eyes like a stricken animal. I could not help but be reminded of the road to Calvary — the heavy load, the whipping and the wounds . . . I led her to the side of the road, took the heavy yoke from her and slung it as far as I could. This action must have been unprecedented for the spirit man did not know what to do at first; he then forget his role as the 'spirit' and spoke to me. He said that he was taking her to the chief, so I told him to go and tell the chief what had happened.

I yelled for one of the boys — there was only one on the compound — he came with some water for the old women, who had collapsed completely by then. Her pulse was almost non-existent. She had been walking like this, in the blazing sun with this heavy load, the juju lashing at her back, for five miles. How she survived I'll never know.

Before we could rouse her sufficiently to take her on to our compound, the chief was there with a lot more juju men, but also quite a few people from the church, who had heard that there was a palaver. One of the church members was a great help; he told me at once that this was not my business, and I told him to go and read his New Testament again. The rest (of the Christians) were one hundred percent with me but a wee bit scared of the chief. He ranted and raved, said this woman was a witch and was the cause of the cholera!

The idea was to put her on trial. I remained adamant and, by the grace of God, they did not try to take her by force, as they could so easily have done. I was told that I would be reported to the District Head, and that, if the sickness came to Kanyehu I would be held responsible; then they stormed off.

I put the woman into a house on the compound and went to see the District Head. He said that he had not told them to beat her, though he had told them to try her. He said I should tell the chief to leave the woman with me and the juju should not enter my compound at all.

We came back to find it was too late — they had entered the house and taken her. A youngster, left on the compound, had heard them suggest that they force her to 'drink plenty'; this meant to pour and pour water until she could not swallow and would drown! Off I went to the scene of the 'trial'.

She was half-sitting, half-sprawling, in an open space surrounded by a couple of hundred men. A juju man behind her, whip in hand, beat her every time she went to fall, or if she failed to answer up as they wanted. I told the chief what the District Head had said, and that I had taken photographs of his men beating the old woman along the way; that, if she died, I would send the pictures to Keffi as evidence against them.

"Why are you treating this poor old lady like this?" I demanded.

"Because she has caused the cholera," the chief responded.

"So this is your treatment for cholera?"

"Yes," replied the chief.

"Right," said I, "if cholera comes to your compound don't come to me for treatment."

"You mean you would not give any?"

"No, you've taken your treatment."

"Stop beating her!" ordered the chief hastily.

The old woman fell to the ground and stretched out her hand to me so pathetically.

I could not get her away, and had to content myself with saying that if I did not see her on my compound that night in no worse condition than now, there was going to be trouble. I have to laugh at it in retrospect, but it sure proves that one with God is a majority!

Well, later that evening Snoopy barked and barked, and when I went to investigate I found the old lady collapsed on the other side of the compound. We put her in the house for the night. She made a remarkable recovery — full of cuts and bruises, of course, but her general condition was remarkable. The staff here were so good to her in giving her food and generally caring for her.

I had a deputation of chiefs up in the evening (Sunday), representing all the tribes. The idea was to make me say that I was sorry for my deeds; so I told them that I did not want to interfere with their 'custom', but if I saw the same thing happening, I would take the same action. After some more conversation they got around to 'thanking' me for taking her, for had they killed her there would have been a palaver with the Government.

They asked me to take her out of the area; dear love them, they still think she is the cause of the cholera!

Of course I had every intention of getting her away, and today tried to put her on a lorry but not one would take her. No woman would look at her because she herself is 'taboo' now. So I took her in my car about twenty miles away to a village where she says she has a sister. I had her on the floor of the car and let her out where there was no-one to see, for the story is bound to have travelled by bush telegraph, and I did not want her associated with me in this new village lest it identify her.

She was amazed at the trouble we had all taken - Japheth brought her some porridge this morning (the seller would not sell it to her directly) and put sugar on it. The poor old dear kept saying wonderingly, "Today I tasted porridge with sugar!" We told her why we did it, and of the One who had done so much more, suffering even more than she, willingly for our sake. She seemed to understand, said she will never make sacrifice again and will try to learn more. We pray that this whole unhappy incident may yet have fruit to His glory. No one, apart from the Christians, can understand why I should care.

Although this report shows how strongly Gwen could react to customs which were so cruel and contrary to her understanding of love, she was not unaware, nor unsympathetic to the pagan society regarding the dilemma posed by the advance of civilisation and Christianity. An article she wrote in 'Dispatch' magazine under the heading of "The Sacred Tree", bears this out:

One Sunday in the early 1970s, worshippers coming from the morning service at the Qua Iboe Church at Kanyehu encountered a congregation of a very different sort. At the foot of a large tree, just off the church compound, stood a group of men, one of whom was leading a small goat which he tethered to a nearby bush. Their obvious leader was an old man whose poverty was apparent in his ragged clothing. With hands outstretched in pleading, he approached the tree and in a voice full of supplication, proceeded to beseech its spirit for the much-needed rain.

After a time, strips of cloth were pinned to the tree, adding to those already there. Further supplication was made and wine poured out as an oblation; then the goat was brought forward, its throat cut and the blood liberally splattered on and around the tree. The whole ceremony was so real to the participants that one's heart ached for them and their futile trust in an unseeing, unhearing, uncaring 'god'. If only they might know Him who created that very tree.

Year by year this procedure is carried out at several such trees in the area, and many goats are sacrificed in a desperate attempt to bring rain. If the desired rainfall does not come it does not seem to affect their faith. Rather they take the blame upon themselves and redouble their efforts, in spite of the increasing cost of the goats they offer.

In 1978 a different kind of activity took place in the vicinity of the old tree. Work on the long-talked-of tarred road between Toto and Umaisha had actually begun. Surveyors had already marked the route of the road, which was to be twenty-four feet wide and involved the destruction of some houses and encroachment on many compounds. The sacred tree was among numerous others earmarked for felling.

As the bulldozers approached there was great apprehension in the hearts of the pagan people. At first they asserted boldly that no machine could ever knock this tree down. As the big machine rolled on, clearing others away as though they were matchsticks, their confidence wavered and they said, "Even if it falls, it will rise again."

Many people from all communities — Moslems, Christian and pagan — gathered to watch as the time came for the tree to be dealt with. By now the tune had changed again to, "If this tree is felled then seven people will surely die."

Powers of evil are very real and we felt that prayer should be made for the protection of the machine operators and others involved in the work. Some trees had resisted the bulldozers and this one, being taller and greater in girth, was expected to be troublesome. However, it must have had comparatively shallow roots for it fell at the first attempt.

When other trees fell, people had swarmed over them like ants, using their axes and gleefully piling up firewood. Not so with this tree. The pagan priests had prophesied doom for any who touched it. Then came the timber company with electric saw and chains. The object of so much sacrifice and worship was sawn to pieces, the useful parts taken away and the remainder pushed off the road to rot in the bush.

Much is heard these days about what is termed a political vacuum. In situations such as this in Bassa, the sweeping away of old things is creating a spiritual vacuum, like that portrayed by the Lord Jesus in Matthew 12:43-45. How we need to pray that these bewildered people may be introduced to Him and that, within the church, good and able teachers may be raised up to fill this vacuum with the indestructable Truth of God!

When Gwen went on leave for a well-earned rest she had plenty of stories to tell. Regularly she would have her audience in fits of laughter as she described the bizarre incidents of everyday life in Bassa, with the slant of her own comical view of things. Often the joke was on her, and no one was more amused than she if that were so. But, because her own heart was deeply touched, she could prod deep into the hearts of her hearers too, and laughter would readily turn to soft compassion, leading to earnest prayer for a people in as great need of Christ as we ourselves, yet with so meagre an opportunity.

A number of church groups and individuals gave her prayer backing, with Syon Mission Church, Brentford embracing her and her work as their own. Pastor Ivor Herbert was a particular blessing to Gwen; writing regularly to encourage her when she was abroad; sharing her burdens and frustrations; taking up her cause when he felt she needed it. When she was at home, he and the fellowship at Syon, spared nothing to provide for her needs and pastoral care. Gwen was able to say with absolute sincerity, "If it were not for my pastor and my church, I would not be able to go on."

Then, there was her close friendship with Valerie Luff; a bond which had developed since Bible college days. They were able to take their U.K. leaves at the same time. Gwen from Nigeria, Valerie from Pakistan, often arriving at Heathrow the very same day. Their weeks together were full of joy and laughter. Each seemed to rejuvenate the other in appreciation of life and of matters spiritual. Because they both worked in particularly 'hard' places, they were able to share each other's burdens with an exceptional degree of understanding. Neither ever visited the other's field of service, but each had a very firm foot of faith planted in the other's 'land'.

Songs were never far from their lips. When they bought the joint home in Icklesham it reverberated with laughter, song and praise. Travelling by car, often the whole journey would be a service of sung delight in the Lord. The songs, which renewed people everywhere were singing, were a great joy to Gwen and Val and they took great delight in teaching them to others. The author remembers when travelling with Gwen on two occasions, one in the west of England and one in Bassa, how she would sing one lovely song after another; often prefixing it with the words, "Have you heard this one?" or "Here's a lovely song."

Her Lord Jesus was becoming more captivatingly real to her and to Val. They went about the country together, or separately on their deputation work; the sweet fragrance of the presence of their Lord enveloping them and those they met.

CHAPTER 7

The Craftsman at Work

As Gwen grew in her relationship with her Father, so her attitude to people softened noticeably. She realised with regret that her zeal had often led her to speak too sharply; a fact that some of her fellow-workers had experienced, to their pain. Her tongue was not spiteful, however, it was just that injustice, or inefficiency, caused her indignation to rise. But she would listen carefully to the other point of view and often accept it, never holding a grudge, easily forgiving. One of her favourite sayings was, "Be patient with me. God hasn't finished with me yet!"

As the work of the Holy Spirit reached deeper into her life, the outward joy began to be matched by an inner peace, and she became a great peacemaker. When she accepted responsibility on the Field executive she was a wise counsellor, both from the basis of experience, and scripture. She once said that now that she was facing the problems of leadership she saw how much more difficult it was than she had previously realised. "If I had known I would not have been so critical. I think it would be good for everyone to try their hand at this!"

With very few exceptions the church in Bassa was far from encouraging. Here too, Gwen found that the work of the Holy Spirit within mellowed her attitude. Not that she became blind to the faults, nor cynical about the possibility of change, but rather more hopeful in God, whose church it is after all. She had a vivid dream in which she was attacked by a large dog which was muzzled. Gwen held in her arms a baby which she fought to protect. The dog tried to get at the baby and succeeded in knocking Gwen down but the baby was unharmed. She saw this as a picture of the devil attempting to devour the infant Bassa church. Significantly, she felt a protective attitude towards it, and was ready to suffer on its behalf. She would, in fact, soon have to give her all to Bassa.

There was, currently, much talk in missionary circles about 'job description,' 'specific limited tasks,' and such like. Gwen would have embraced such ideas at one time, but no longer. She was here to serve the Lord in whatever He asked and she would do so gladly and without question. He could be trusted not to ask more of His child than He would give grace to meet.

In the lonely times, when fellowship was unavailable, Gwen found the use of tapes a great help. Some of the splendid teaching tapes by well-known ministers were sent out to her, and a regular supply of her own Pastor's messages from Syon. These, together with a good helping of hymns and spiritual songs, were her diet on many occasions, in place of conventional worship in God's house.

She prayed aloud. She found this a very positive help, both to concentration, and to the increased reality of God's presence. She gave herself to praise, accepting the scriptural principle of praise IN all things, but rejecting the popular idea of praise FOR all things. The difference here, she felt, was very important: not all things were good, but God would make all things work together for her good.

There was at Sardauna a beautifully built mission centre with a small dispensary, supervised by the Sudan Interior Mission and the Evangelical Church of West Africa (E.C.W.A.). The S.I.M. asked the Q.I.M. to take over this work, with the twenty or so churches, when they no longer had anyone to staff it. David and Léon moved the thirty-seven miles from Kanyehu to this new responsibility whilst Gwen and Lily continued at Kanyehu, with Meta Dunlop filling in during leaves.

When, at last, official permission was received, Eric Kerr returned to Kanyehu with his family to build the new dispensary. For weeks the compound became a builder's yard of sand, stone, blocks and timber. With extraordinary speed the purpose-built structure took shape. It had, of course, taken five years from the first verbal approval, and would take many more months before the official inspection would pronounce it 'above standard', and legal use could be made of it.

A large gift through T.E.A.R. Fund covered almost all the building costs, and another generous gift from women in Northern Ireland supplied most of the equipment. Gwen was now seeing her vision taking shape. Soon the gap between the privileged and the deprived of this world would be closed, but by the smallest degree, at Kanyehu.

On the south side of the Benue river, the work, started years ago by some of the Qua Iboe pioneers had now passed into the hands of Robert and Joyce Hyslop, who, though warmly associated with Q.I.M. were, nevertheless, independent. It was a great joy always for the missionaries from the north to get together with the Hyslops, whose bright faith and 'warm' home were an inspiration. Gwen and Lily began spending their Christmases with the Hyslops, as well as paying numerous visits whever they passed that way.

The Lord was beginning to pour out a special blessing on this work on the south bank. Not only were many converted and some healed in the services, but the presence of God was being experienced in extraordinary ways so that hidden sin was being forced into the open and confessed, often with tears. Reconciliations between brothers long separated was a heartening feature, and a strong, wise leadership was emerging in the churches.

The Hyslops themselves and those close to them at Odenyi were filled with the Holy Spirit and joy. Gwen revelled in their fellowship and longed for the blessing she saw here to cross the river and set fire to the church there. She, in a personal way, was to feel gratitude for this blessing. One day, unable to hide her back pain from Joyce, she was asked if she would like specific prayer. Gwen readily accepted. Joyce laid her hands on her and prayed. Gwen returned to Kanyehu where, for a week, the agony continued unabated. It was then that, whilst at work in the dispensary, she felt a jolt and heard a loud crack At first she was afraid to rise from her stool, but when she did she found that she was completely free of pain. The cure was permanent.

When David and Léon visited the Hyslops' home one day on their way to Igala, they were disappointed to find the house empty. However, there was compensation in full measure when they discovered that the first Bassa New Testaments had arrived at last, after a ten-year wait. Ken Williams' heroic work had finally come to fruition.

The 4th May, 1973, was a day of great rejoicing at Odenyi as people gathered to welcome the New Testaments. That day the first heavy rain of the season broke in a deluge over the crowds as they came from far and wide. Nothing could dampen their enthusiasm, though, while they stood in soaked clothing for four joy-filled hours participating in the Service of Thanksgiving. Over eight hundred copies were sold within a few days, and people could be seen everywhere joyfully bearing home their new prize.

One week later, on the north side of the river, the service was repeated with equal zest. How thrilling it was to see with what pleasure they fondled those precious long-awaited books! Old Baba Jonathan looked especially happy, so did Jonah who had assisted with the translation, and Nye Zomo, the tuberculosis patient who was just learning to read.

People in the area were awakening to the value of books. David and Léon found themselves carrying more and more literature for sale and often running out of stock long before the demand was met. Hausa calendars with scripture texts could be seen all over the area in classrooms, churches and homes of every religious leaning. Every day the voice of the gospel was being heard from these silent witnesses; many of them in homes where any other Christian influence would be anathema.

A report by David and Léon on the literature work in its later development spoke of the sale of five thousand calendars and eight hundred New Testaments. Visits were made to many schools, markets and conferences, with dramatic results. Children, wild with excitement, would crowd around, eager to get their hands on the little booklets. At one such school they had spent most of the morning selling to pupils and teachers. At last every customer seemed satisfied and the missionaries drove back down the track through the tall grass which threatened to engulf them. After a mile, out of sight of the school, they stopped for a much needed drink. When they had finished they started the car and began to move on. There was a sound of frantic running and a small boy appeared, panting, perspiring and gasping, "I want book," as if his very life depended on it. The book was supplied, with a bonus — the Griffiths did not have the heart to take the little fellow's money.

Cassette players were proving a useful tool. Lily was able to procure tapes in a number of the local languages and play them to groups in the various compounds. She found that the people listened extra carefully to the messages in their own tongue, and the theme could then be used as a talking point. Christians, too, began to use these machines to record messages at conferences and relay them to their friends and family at home.

If no one was available to speak to the patients at the Kanyehu dispensary Gwen would play a tape to them. She was concerned that they should receive medicine for the soul as well as the body. She often tussled with her conscience over the fact that she did not witness personally to each patient. When it is remembered that in the year '77-'78 she treated sixteen thousand people, it is little wonder she could not spare time to talk to many.

On a certain morning, though, she determined she would speak to each patient, and asked the Lord for guidance to the fertile ground. Gwen tells the story herself:

> June 1977. The third woman I spoke to told me she knew why God had urged me to speak to her. As a child she had been interested in the gospel but, belonging to a Moslem household, she was married to a Moslem husband. She is

from the Igbirra tribe and now seems to have made a very real decision. The family are antagonistic and she is prepared to be sent away by her husband but says she can't deny the Lord any longer. Do please pray for her.

September 1977. I had a visit from Adama yesterday. At the beginning she had asked me about going to church and I left it entirely to herself, knowing this would increase her trouble. Now she tells me that she attended church on her own in Umaisha on Sunday, which is a very big step for her to take. Opposition is increasing. Even the family where she waits after receiving medicines until I am free to chat with her, have now said that if she insists on being a believer then she is not welcome to visit them any more. Her own family have told her husband to send her home to them and threaten to beat her to her senses. She just says, "Even if they kill me it will make no difference." At least two other women of the same tribe have suffered real physical hardship for the same cause.

January 1978. Adama's husband has carried out his threat to send her to her people in Shafan Abakwa. She went completely unperturbed, in fact rejoicing because the services there are conducted in her own Igbirra tongue! She is just thrilled to think she might get the opportunity to have fellowship with her own tribe and listen to the Word of God in her own language. The beating to her is just incidental; it does not worry her a bit, which really puts US to shame, doesn't it?

She is completely illiterate and has so little fellowship. There is not one other Igbirra Christian in Umaisha. At the dispensary I was careful not to draw attention to her but one day when I was preaching she was chatting away to the women. The boys (dispensary assistants) told me afterwards that she was saying she had heard this message for a long time and had resisted, but now she had received it. She advised them to do the same because one did not know how long the opportunity would be given. So there she is — witnessing already! I saw her again just last Friday and she was radiant.

Over at Sardauna the medical work was reopened with the help of several nurses who came and went as they could be spared from other places. Margaret Langridge found that there were hardly enough patients coming to keep her busy, the people preferring to continue with their own brews and local 'doctors'.

At the hub of a network of many small villages, Sardauna's main problem was access. The only route into the mission centre, ten miles long, was appalling. Long stretches of deep sand made traction impossible. Washed-out gullies and broken bridges in ever-changing patterns caused concern for the driver every time a journey had to be made. Many of the villages around could only be reached on foot. When Meta and Margaret held the fort there they spent quite a lot of their time visiting the villages and schools. They found opportunity to teach Bible Knowledge classes at both Toto and Adadu schools, enjoying excellent discipline and attentiveness among the pupils.

These two nurses had a dramatic start to their time at Sardauna. Unknown to them the rubber hose connecting the gas stove to the supply cylinder had perished. Happily there was no one in the house when an explosion occurred and the room was set ablaze. The fire was brought under control eventually, though it had caused a considerable amount of damage. When Gwen heard about it she made one of her typical quips, "Those two certainly started off with a bang!"

Margaret Langridge wrote in the mission magazine about the work at Sardauna:

> In Psalm 48 verse 2 the city of our God is described as being "beautiful in situation". When I suggested to a colleague that the same could be said of Sardauna she thought it was most amusing. She had heard it called many things before but never that! Seen in the setting of the surrounding hills the Mission House is indeed in a beautiful situation, but the difficulty experienced in travelling detracts somewhat from the beauty of the

country. Some of the roads are not too bad in dry weather but in the wet season it can be a very different story.

Imagine waking up one morning at 3 a.m. to a violent thunderstorm, knowing that today is the day you are supposed to be travelling to Igala. At 5 a.m. it is still raining hard. The arrangement is to meet our fellow missionaries at Adadu, ten miles away, at 7 a.m., in order to travel with them to a Prayer Day at Ochadamu. Faced with 'that road' our hearts nearly fail us, but 5.30 a.m. sees us setting off, walking and pushing the Honda. It's dark, still raining hard, and we wonder if we have gone completely mad.

Dawn begins to break and the rain is falling less heavily. We can at least see where we are going now so decide to try the Honda. Between riding some of the time and walking over the bad patches we eventually come within a mile of Adadu, having had our faces washed en route by the tall grass now heavy with the rain.

So we come to THE hill. It's steep and badly rutted. Added to that, it's now wet and muddy, and very slippery. There's no question of riding so we get off and try to get ourselves and the bike up it. About a quarter of the way up the bike gets stuck in a rut and it takes a lot of heaving and pushing to get it out and up the last stretch. At the top we pause awhile to regain our breath (we MUST be getting old!) before riding into Adadu. We are three-quarters of an hour late and very relieved to hear our colleagues have not yet passed through. It's great to get a cup of coffee and the breakfast we had no time to finish, having left so much earlier than intended because of the rain. Was it worth it? We think so. The presence of the Lord was very real with us on our Day of Prayer and Mr. Dickson's message on the 'Second Watch' a great blessing to us all.

In two of the villages near here a number of people have been turning to Christ recently. Meta and I decided to visit one of these, where about fourteen young people of the Gwari tribe have repented. Tomua is five miles away and we ask the Christians in Sardauna how to get there. "Can we take the Honda?" Hoots of laughter greet this suggestion, accompanied by much stamping of feet to indicate that the only way there is to walk. They promise us one young boy to show the way. So at 7.30 a.m. the following Sunday morning we set off. The first mile is fine, though only a track, but the going soon became much rougher. We find ourselves climbing downhill to a stream, splashing our way through and then clambering up the other side. When you've done that four or five times you begin to realise why they thought it so funny when we suggested taking the bike! When we weren't clambering up and down hills we were walking along paths flanked on either side by grass, taller than ourselves and gently waving in the breeze; the sort of country where you would expect to see a herd of elephants come ponderously along. In fact, the only 'wild life' that we saw, apart from birds and butterflies, was a solitary millipede on the path.

After asking our guide several times if we were anywhere near to Tomua, we came to a place where the path went through a farm with guinea corn growing high on either side. Soon the village came into view. The villagers greeted us warmly, but imagine how we felt to learn that the Christians had gone to another village to preach! At the same time, how it thrilled us to find these young Christians already witnessing for the Lord. The people assured us they would soon be back, so we sat down to wait. Half an hour later we could hear them coming, singing the praises of the Lord. After travelling they were hungry, so first of all had a meal. That over, at 11 a.m., we gathered under the shade of a tree to have our service, for they have only just started to build their own little mud church. About twenty young folk gathered, with a few older ones sitting at a distance listening.

There were two blind people in the village: one a middle-aged woman, the other a teenage boy. The boy had such a lost, hopeless look on his face and he was wandering about aimlessly. One felt so sorry for him, yet is he not a picture of a soul without Christ? Pray that those in Tomua and the many other villages who are spiritually blind may soon be able to say, "One thing I know, that though I was blind now I see." Pray too for those who are already His, that the living Word of God may continue to grow and prosper among them.

At a village two miles from Sardauna was an old lady who had been converted just four years. She had almost no fellowship nor teaching, but faithfully continued with the Lord. A tiny grass-roofed shelter served as the church. Each Sunday this woman went and sat there, nearly always alone, and prayed. She was unable to read and knew only a few Christian songs. When Margaret and Meta arrived at her village, one Sunday, she was overjoyed to see them. The great need for such isolated believers was for some Christians from the larger churches to forfeit their own services and go to fellowship with the lonely, sharing with them out of their abundance.

Women's Fellowship Conferences became a heartening feature. These were held at various centres three or four times annually. Many women travelled long distances to meet with their sisters in Christ, to warm each other's faith and to share the Good News among their neighbours. Writing about the witness of these women Léon Griffiths paints the picture:

The early sun cast long shadows on this cool, fresh Sunday morning. Few people were about as a happy chattering group of women and girls entered the second compound and gathered before a house where several people were talking. The women had walked from the neighbouring village of Sardauna where the Women's Conference was in progress. They had come this morning in response to a plea of a Christian — "Come and witness in my village."

As they paused, deciding what to sing, a man appeared with a calabash of palm wine, with which he drenched the ju-ju shrine before the house where the women stood. Then a goat was brought to be sacrificed. Somebody started to sing and everyone took up the strain.

"Weeping, work . . . prayer . . . even the sacrifice of goats and cocks will not save us — only faith in Christ . . . His blood poured out for me."

The blood of the goat poured out and was daubed liberally over the crude mud altar. The women continued singing the Bassa version of the hymn, "Alas and did my Saviour bleed."

What a picture! Now a smartly-clad Bassa woman, with a fine bearing and an earnest look on her open face, stepped boldly forward to explain about the true sacrifice. The contrast was amazing: a woman confidently trusting in the finished work of Christ and men vainly trying to placate the spirits. As we contemplate this picture of light and darkness, let the challenge which came to Paul come to us: "I send thee to open their eyes, and to turn them from darkness to light, and from the power of Satan unto God, that they may receive forgiveness of sins and an inheritance among them which are sanctified by faith which is in me."

We praise the Lord for everyone who attended the conference. Six schoolgirls walked thirty-five miles from Kanyehu to be present and sang at all the sessions. Four girls came over the hills from Tomo where some Gwaris are trusting the Lord. Other women came twelve miles from Toto, some from nearer places, making a total of twenty-seven. Please give God the glory for the work He is doing and pray that the Holy Spirit will continue to work.

Each year, just after Christmas, as many as possible of the Qua Iboe missionaries would gather together for a time of refreshing and prayer. These retreats were often times of great renewing of soul and vision for the work. Ochadamu Medical Centre, in Igala, was a favourite spot; the peaceful, open park-like area seemed ideal surroundings for meditation and quiet. However, to afford a change for the Ochadamu staff, the retreat was held at the Ochaja Secondary Schools occasionally, and later, at the lovely Miango Rest House, high up on the Jos Plateau.

When it was suggested, one year, that the retreat be held at Kanyehu, it was not Gwen alone who questioned the wisdom of this. Excessively hot and dusty; lacking accommodation and short of water, remote and difficult of access, and no large team of people to arrange matters, Kanyehu seemed a bad choice. Despite all this, bravely the challenge was accepted and on the day appointed the influx of white visitors descended upon the village and mission centre.

The retreat itself proved to be a time of rich fellowship and, when Sunday came, the blessing spilled over into the local church. A host of people came to Kanyehu because of the novelty of so many white visitors. The church had never been so full. The village chief came, and he, with many other non-Christians, heard the gospel clearly preached that day.

Rarely, if ever, would there be so many of Gwen's colleagues at Kanyehu again. When they left, the place seemed extra lonely. But there were visitors from time to time and these were always made most welcome. The fact that Gwen's local supermarket was about two hundred and fifty miles away made such catering a little more than difficult. The only fresh meat available nearby was stewing beef. When a group of Q.I.M. missionaries from the south descended on Gwen for a few days the Lord provided an unexpected treat. The neighbourhood hunter appeared at Gwen's door with a guinea fowl which he kindly presented as a gift.

When, some weeks later, a group of S.I.M. friends arrived, Gwen asked the hunter if he could possibly supply another fowl. He came — with a whole antelope! One of the Americans among the visitors commiserated with Gwen, "Just be grateful that he did not meet up with an elephant!" Staff, visitors and school teachers lived on venison for a week.

To meet the need for a variation in diet Gwen tried an experiment in keeping rabbits. It was not too successful. She complained that three of the five does would have nothing to do with the buck; 'man-haters' she called them, and threatened to introduce them to the pressure cooker if they continued in their rebellion.

Most visitors came unexpectedly. Not much point trying to telephone Kanyehu. The first indication of a guest arriving would usually be the crunch of tyres outside the door. David and Léon came often from Sardauna to see that all was well with Gwen, but one occasion was special. As their car drew up at Gwen's house they could be heard singing at the top of their voices, like people just out of a beer parlour: "Happy birthday to Gwen; only five days till then." They piled out of their car with their arms full of goodies for a feast, and together they had a somewhat premature celebration.

African roads are dangerous. Paradoxically, when new roads take the place of the old pot-holed tracks, there is no lessening of the danger because the traffic simply goes faster. An old lorry might lumber slowly along the bush highways without coming to grief, but when the driver, often a young lad, sees before him a stretch of blacktop he puts the pedal to the floor. If the steering arm drops off, or a front tyre bursts, the resulting accident is horrifying.

Gwen had her share of accident victims to attend. A motor-cycle with a woman pillion rider nose-dives off the side of a bridge on to the rock-hard dry river bed. Concussion and multiple injuries result. People are carried in to the dispensary with broken bones, bruises, deep wounds and in shock. Motor-cycles, now taking the place of push bikes, are the cause of most injuries.

Valerie Green came to Bassa for a brief visit with Sunday, the driver from Ochadamu. Their purpose was to bring Norah Curran back to Igala. The road they used was new, though some work was still in progress. There was a clear run through on a good surface. Next morning at 5 a.m. Gwen bid Norah, Valerie and Sunday farewell and prepared for her day's work. Five hours later a message came to the effect that an accident had happened.

With some trepidation Gwen set out. After only sixteen miles she found them sitting despondently at the side of the road in a car which would take some repairing. Valerie had a deep cut over the eye and Norah was badly shaken, but Sunday was suffering from indignation. He had been driving, just before daylight, on a road which, only a few hours before, had been clear. Now the whole road was blocked with a huge pile of earth dumped from a lorry by a road worker who obviously had no idea of the hazard he had created. When Gwen stitched Valerie's wounds she was not sure which of them suffered more.

The opening up of the country by the new major highways, affected Kanyehu considerably more than most other places, because the new Federal Capital was planned to be sited just north of the Benue. When the road was built between Umaisha and the new capital it passed right through the mission compound at Kanyehu, effectively cutting it in two. Gwen found that her side of the compound ended up four metres above the road surface. The contractors had to install a flight of steps for her to descend, cross the road and climb to the dispensary side. "Ah, well," she sighed, "it keeps me fit!"

Massive bridges were under construction also and when they were completed, hours were cut from journeys which had previously entailed using ferries. In particular, the journey to Igala, to link up with other Qua Iboe Missionb staff, was made easier and the sense of isolation slightly lessened.

Thieves and bandits soon caught on to the benefits afforded to their trade by the coming of the highways. The hitherto remote villages were not thief conscious. Their customs, taboos and close-built communities made stealing generally unacceptable. But the coming of strangers through the area in great numbers opened new harvests for those with an eye to theft; moreover the fast roads made it easy to put sufficient distance between burglar and crime before ever the loss was discovered.

People with items worth stealing began to employ armed guards to protect their property. That these security men spent a great deal of their time asleep was no problem: provided it was known that a guard was on duty it was supposed that no thief would take the risk of being ventilated with buckshot. When well-meaning neighbours asked Gwen if she had guards on the compound, she replied with a twinkling of eye, "Certainly! I have three guards very well armed: the Father, the Son and the Holy Spirit."

Had she not had faith in God she would not have come to Nigeria in the first instance, but by the practice of faith in everyday experiences, her understanding of faith's reality became a solid foundation upon which she could work. She could ask for rain to fill her empty water tanks and receive a downpour enough to last for several weeks. Then, the same day, in full knowledge that the bush paths would be washed out and treacherous, she would ask for dry roads to a certain place where she simply had to go alone. Three miles from Kanyehu the roads would be dust dry.

This does not mean that she always had answers to her prayers just as she prayed them. In common with all God's children she had to learn to wait for some answers and to accept God's 'No' to some requests. Where faith came in here was in believing not FOR an answer but IN the Father who always knows best. In fact she often used this very term when things seemed to go awry, "Father knows best."

CHAPTER 8

The Refining

Changes were coming to Bassa at an accelerating rate. Musa, who had rebelled and turned to wrong in the past, had now set up a rival church in Kanyehu, much to the confusion of the local people and to Gwen's sorrow. However, the Lord was gracious in this also because, undoubtedly, some found blessing through this church; and Gwen had many a useful talk with Musa.

When Noah and Grace returned to live in the area, Gwen and Lily were delighted to renew fellowship with them. As often as possible they visited this couple's home en route to the post office, eighty miles away. Grace, expecting their eighth child, was eager after the birth to get involved with Lily in the work of Women's Fellowship. Talk of this was never far from the surface when the ladies were together and there was considerable excitement as plans began to take shape.

On the 18th February, 1981, Grace told Lily that she hoped to take an active part in the Easter Women's Conference. On the 19th while leading the Women's Fellowship Meeting in the local church she became ill with a complication related to the birth. Noah was away from home, and a long delay occurred before Grace was moved to Keffi Hospital. The baby died and Grace did not survive surgery. This must have been a devastating blow to Noah, added to which was the care of seven children. Even so, in his first grief, he was able to testify to the love of God being very real. The question as to why such a thing should happen defies an answer, but, as Noah said to the stricken Gwen and Lily, "We cannot argue with God."

The churches in the area surrounding Sardauna had opted to return to the care of E.C.W.A., and David and Léon Griffiths were given a new appointment, to open up a literature work based at Ugwolawo in Igala. This proved to be perfect timing by the Lord, for the literacy rate of the nation had created a hunger for books of such vast proportions that the Good News book van was in constant use. The faster the books were ordered the faster they sold, and by no means only to Christians.

At Umaisha was a Moslem Secondary School started and run by a Moslem group from Pakistan called Ahmadiyya. In accordance with Nigerian laws on freedom of religion, Christians could attend this school if they wished without being subject to Islamic indoctrination. A Fellowship of Christian Students was commenced early in the life of the school and this became a means of encouragement to the students. A number of the missionaries from Kanyehu and Sardauna were invited to speak at the F.C.S. from time to time and strong links were forged. Later Gwen and Lily also took regular classes in Religious Knowledge, which, of course, the Moslem teachers were unable to supply for the Christians.

Gwen found the Pakistani and Sri Lankan families delightful. Sometimes she was called to attend to their medical needs; at others it was on a more social level that they met; eating together in one another's houses. It was a special joy for Gwen to find among them a Christian Sri Lankan, Rita Paul, wife of one of the teachers; they became fast friends. Though the student population changed from year to year, Gwen got to know many of them very well and they looked upon her as their mother in the faith, often bringing their problems to her sympathetic ear.

The new road was at last completed after a series of contractors of various nations had come and gone. It was great to have the tar right up to the door. The construction crews, together with their gigantic machinery, used the mission compound as a base for several months. The only adjective Gwen could find to describe this experience was 'interesting'.

Helpers in the dispensary had changed over the years. Some would move on to further training, others could not stand the pace of the work, and a few had to be dismissed for dishonesty. In June 1981 Gwen wrote home about the present helpers and the attacks from the enemy they experienced:

Andrew has now gone for training and we are 'doing by manage' with Isaac and Hannah — Andrew's wife. She works just part-time. Ruth, Isaac's wife, had a baby girl in March. During her pregnancy she had a very bad time contending with 'voices' which told her she would die if she stayed on the compound. It is a long story, but suffice it to say that after a period when she was quite beside herself and unable to be reasoned with, during which she left Isaac and returned to her people, she did return again and each time these voices bothered her, Isaac counteracted by reading the Word of God to her and praying.

Her premature labour caused a bit of concern but we clearly see the hand of God in this now and just praise Him. The baby was small though healthy but it was a difficult birth and I'm convinced that had the baby not been so small Ruth could have been in real trouble. Since the birth of the child she has been much more stable and responsive. However, a couple of weeks ago there was an incident which upset her considerably.

Lily and I were sleeping when the most terrified screams came from the staff quarters. Hannah, Ruth and Isaac were there . . . Hannah was quiet but afraid. Ruth was still screaming. Isaac was quiet by the time we got there but obviously shaken. In reply to our question it seems that they were sitting chatting when Ruth looked over Isaac's shoulder and said someone was coming. He thought it was a patient, glanced casually behind him and saw what he described as "a dark form coming out of the darkness, with the face of death." He leapt to his feet to get his torch (it was about 10.45 p.m.) and suddenly fell to the ground, completely helpless and terribly cold . . . This is when he shouted in terror, although he has no recollection of it. We ourselves saw nothing. Some of the nearby Christians came up and asked if we had been able to smell anything, but we hadn't.

Since then Isaac and Hannah have seemingly been able to commit this to the Lord and are alright. Ruth is still very fearful, though mostly on account of her baby. Just before I came on holiday she and Isaac had gone away for a weekend; she to her people, he to his. He returned on the Sunday evening, but when I came away the following Friday, Ruth and the baby had still not returned, so we are just praying that she will not give in to this spirit of fear but may trust in the Lord and know the spirit of "power, love and a sound mind."

The church was sorely in need of strong leadership. After considerable difficulty over the correct choice, four elders had been ordained, three Bassas and one Igbirra: Paul, David, Jonathan and Jonah. These men were finding the churches no easier to guide than had the missionaries; in fact, their closer links through family and tribe made it harder for them to exercise discipline when needed.

With the help of the Igala church, several men were sent to the Qua Iboe Church Bible College at

Ankpa for training, with the idea that they would return to serve the churches of Bassa. Some of these did fulfil their promise, but others used the opportunity to take teaching posts in primary schools, thus ensuring for themselves a much higher salary than the church could afford.

It became the 'in' thing for young people to break with the old animistic customs. The incompatibility of education and paganism caused a rift between parents and children: the former becoming angry and confused by the new ideas, and the latter being provocatively high-handed with their elders. By no means all who turned from paganism went over to another religion; some became more materialistic than their western counterparts. But many simply did drift into the churches without an awareness of any need for salvation, repentance or renewal. The consequent dilution of spiritual life gave Satan many a new opportunity to drain away the high standards set by early dependence on the Truth of God, though at the same time many more were hearing the gospel.

Bible Students from Ankpa and the Samuel Bill Theological College at Abak visited Bassa on their annual treks. The enthusiasm and deep spiritual commitment of these students was a challenge to the lethargy of some Bassa believers, but it was also a shock to some of the students from the south to find so backward a place in their modern nation, and so weak a church. Most Nigerians are used to very large churches, packed to the doors and vibrant with life.

One of the students who made up the team was David Udoudom. His few days in Bassa had a profound effect upon him. When he returned to college to complete his course, Bassa was not far from his thoughts: was God calling him to be a missionary to this remote and difficult area?

David had been brought up in the Ibesit area of southern Nigeria, a stark contrast to the Benue basin. The heavy rainfall, overcast skies, humid atmosphere and countless palm trees in his homeland made Bassa's scorching barrenness appear particularly inhospitable to the young man. Then, too, there was his father to consider: an old man now, still involved with paganism and with two wives; he could not be expected to view his son's intentions with enthusiasm. Also, David was in the process of building a house for himself within his father's compound. Would not God be honoured best if he stayed to complete this task?

A more immediate consideration for David was the welfare of his wife, Comfort, and his children. How would Comfort fare in Bassa? How would his children receive an adequate education? Should he take them with him, or leave them with relatives at home? These questions, so familiar to prospective foreign missionaries, taxed the mind and will of this Nigerian for some considerable time. At last, though, he made his approach to the Qua Iboe Church Authorities and asked their confirmation of his call. They gave it gladly.

Before taking his present course at the Samuel Bill Theological College, David had served as a missionary to the Mid-west. This experience would stand him in good stead, but he was under no illusions that his training and experience alone were sufficient for the new task. He needed a deep relationship with his Father and an anointing of the Holy Spirit if he were to be effective in Bassa's spiritual growth.

Gwen considered the prospect of David Udoudom's coming with great enthusiasm. She felt sure that, although a foreigner almost as much as the overseas workers, David would eventually get closer to the local people than the white outsider ever could. Furthermore, Gwen had met David and had been singularly impressed with the man's insight and spiritual awareness.

At about the same time as David was considering these things before the Lord, another David, deeply involved in Bassa's early development, was approaching the end of his course. On 2nd January 1982, David Gilmore went to be with the Lord. One pioneer had gone, and God was already preparing a new brand of pioneer to take his place. Almost exactly a year later David and Comfort Udoudom arrived, with two of their five children; the three eldest being left at home with an uncle.

After his first few months of service, during which time the family lived in rented accommodation — in a shared house used by a prostitute at Ugya, about ten miles from Kanyehu — David wrote to his supporters in Nigeria and the United Kingdom:

> Greetings in the name of our Saviour and Lord, Jesus Christ! I express my gratitude to all of you who uphold me in your prayers. I arrived at Kanyehu in the night of 24th January 1983. Since then the Lord has successfully led us through different experiences in weather, food, language, culture and the like.
>
> The Bassa field is not all that young, but it needs God-centred leadership. There are sixty churches now in the districts, with only three full-time preachers and one branch Bible School teacher. What are these to sixty congregations? Pray with us that God may call workers into His vineyard and give me the much-needed wisdom and patience in both organisation and leadership. I hope to draw up a programme to involve all Christians who can preach, to minister the Word of God to these hungry souls. Pray that God should lead this programme, and bless us and use those involved, to work out good to all.

We are happy to be used by God in our own little efforts to cater for His flock here. My family is divided in two: three children in Cross River State and two here with us. It is a pity to be separated when these teenagers need us most. This is a thorn in the flesh to us, to use Paul's language, but God who gave Paul grace to endure will do the same to both them and us. I am beginning to think of a more useful means of transport which may bring them to stay with us each holiday, so that we may be able to minister to them and discharge our parental duties and share our love with them. Pray that God, in His own way and time, may do His will in this matter.

The main problem is language. Hausa helps me to do shopping and converse in some situations, but we have only one church that uses Hausa in worship; all the rest use Bassa. With the New Testament in Bassa and the Bassa hymnbook, the tendency is to make Bassa the official language in meetings, and I don't even understand the basic greetings yet. Pray that He who equipped the apostles at Pentecost may open our ears and tongues to hear and speak Bassa for a more effective ministry.

As the first flush of his welcome to Bassa wore off, and the involved problems within the church and community began to weigh upon David, he made his way often to Kanyehu in search of fellowship and prayer support. That this was natural, and that Gwen and Lily's reciprocation of confidence was just as natural, will be easily understood by those who are acquainted with the situation. But, in retrospect, this would appear to have been a mistake: drawing David away from the church and towards the mission compound. There can be little doubt that the local people noticed this trend.

However, David certainly put his back into the work, seeking by all means possible to encourage, teach, preach, and, if necessary rebuke; following faithfully in the steps of those who had gone before. Just as his predecessors had suffered disappointment and discouragement, so did he. Satan made sure there were plenty of storms to rock his faith.

To supplement his allowance, David asked the village chief for land to farm. He received an uncharitable refusal. Comfort tried to grow tomatoes but the local lads knocked them down. There were many such annoyances — all part of missionary life — but tedious just the same.

The first major blow fell when the news came from home of his brother's sudden death. Apart from the obvious grief this caused, it also raised some severe problems. David's father would look to him to return home and fill the gap left by his brother, and, this had been the very relative caring for David's three eldest children. It looked like a knockout blow. Prayer was made by a wide circle of friends, and miraculously, David was able to settle matters amicably at home and return to Bassa.

Comfort had her own problems. She had to bring up her family in a totally foreign environment. She struggled to learn the difficult Bassa tongue and used a little Hausa in her marketing. She missed the company of her friends and family in the south, with whom she would have liked to share her frustrations. She felt a warm friendship with Gwen and Lily and drew as close as she could to her neighbours. In the busy life that she led she also tried to make time to accompany her husband on his preaching tours. In every way she was a good helper in the whole ministry of the mission team.

The enemy decided to aim a blow at David through his wife. Gwen wrote in the mission magazine about it:

> 'Danger'. 'Keep out of reach of children'. 'Not to be taken'. Easy for people in the Western hemisphere to take warning of such labels. In an area where all medicines, oils, kerosene, etc., are kept in identical bottles it is not so easy to avoid danger. Nevertheless, the people for the most part are very aware of the danger and have their own way of avoiding it.

When Pastor David had to take drastic action against bedbugs in the new house, it was by use of a powerful D.D.T. solution which proved to be very effective. He stored the bottle with the remains of the insecticide under the bed, but constant questionings from the children as to the contents of the bottle made him seek for another place. No highly-placed bathroom cabinets in this very humble house. So, he put the deadly bottle away at the back of a small cupboard, which contained other bottles — for the most part empty, and one or two with medicines in. On an occasion when he was away from home and one of the children was taken ill, his wife went to the cupboard . . . "Now, which one was the medicine for diarrhoea?" She wasn't one bit sure and wisely decided to give none of them, but to buy more. On the return of the Pastor she told him of her action and received nothing but praise for it . . . So, what went wrong the next time?

Pastor was, as usual, preparing a visit to the bush church. Comfort, his wife, had been unwell all night and needed medication . . . What should she take? As he was telling her to take two spoonfuls of the mixture, someone interrupted and off he went. Two hours afterwards someone from the village arrived at the door of the bush church where he was ministering. "Pastor, your wife is very sick, you have to come . . ." He set off to go and then another from the village arrived on a motor cycle. "Pastor, do not take your own machine, let me carry you . . ." This served to make him very suspicious . . . Why should he be considered unfit to ride? Immediately he questioned the motor cyclist: "You say my wife is very sick, do you mean she is dead? Is that why you do not want me to ride the machine? Please, just tell me the truth. If she is dead, I will ride pillion. If she is alive I will ride pillion. But tell me."

Then came the story: Comfort had carefully measured two spoonfuls of D.D.T. and swallowed it! The narrator had to say reluctantly that he did not think they would find her with life; she had been taken to the health centre in Toto. Into Pastor David's mind came the words ". . . and if they drink any deadly thing it will not hurt them." He clambered on to the machine and set off, singing, "What a friend we have in Jesus." On reaching Toto he saw Comfort lying as one dead — only the faint pulsating in the breast showed that she was in fact still alive. All was panic to get a motor and get her to a 'proper' hospital. Toto hadn't the equipment to cope.

"Before we go running for motor, we are going to pray" — this was her truly devoted husband speaking — and he it was who prayed forthwith.

He went back to their home to get the needed belongings, while others took his wife to hospital. In spite of his confidence in God, his heart was heavy — there was so little sign of life, so little reason for hope. Like a flash the word came again, "able to drink any deadly thing . . ." David recognised this as a Word from the Lord and responded with, "Thank you, dear Lord . . . I trust you."

Then, with his belongings, he got to the hospital. Comfort was in the Lord's care, but how thankful he was to find that there were people here who were able to care for her as well. His dear wife and mother of his five children, to say nothing of foster mother to those of her own dead brother, was conscious that same evening; home two or three days afterwards; and had taken up the reins of the household again before the end of the week! Truly of the Lord.

The whole village is amazed at the fact that Comfort is alive and well. Some refused to believe it was she herself and thought it was her ghost! As a result of the incident, many in the area have seen God's care of His own and acknowledged that He is indeed a living God.

However, Satan had not yet finished his assault on David. Little Item, at five years of age, was full of life and vitality. It was her father, David's brother, who had so recently died. David and Comfort took the child into their own family naturally and gladly. Together with their own children, Item soon settled to the life of Bassa, playing with the local youngsters, hardly aware of language barriers. Very suddenly, Item became ill and died. David and Comfort were grief stricken, as well as beset with doubts regarding the bringing of the child to Bassa in the first place. Perhaps she would have lived had she stayed in the south.

It had only been a few weeks earlier, at the Easter Convention, that David had given a series of messages on 'Christian suffering'. His addresses were delivered with a powerful ring of truth, but now his wonderful attitude of acceptance, and his clear testimony through these trials spoke even more effectively of the grace of God available to the believer.

Despite the rapid changes and development there were some things which seemed to be held in a time-lock. A superficial survey of cities, roads, education and the like, would leave one with the impression of a nation well on the way to completing its ambitious growth programmes, but a short journey down any bush road would reveal another face of Nigeria not much affected by progress. That this is true of any nation, and is part of the appeal of individualism can be appreciated.

When Gwen returned to Kanyehu in February 1984, after "a really lovely furlough", she commented:

> I am happy to be back here for I know this is where the Lord would have me, but I must confess that the heat, dust, responsibility and separation from friends and family all combine to make me feel less than a hundred per cent settled. I had forgotten what it was like to do nothing more strenuous than push a pen and get blinded by perspiration streaming into one's eyes.

Whilst still in the process of unpacking and accepting a handover of responsibility Gwen was again thrown in at the deep end. A ten-year-old lad named Samson had lit a fire in a room where a motor cycle was stored. The petrol tank exploded, the house was burnt down and the boy suffered second and third degree burns all over his back. In spite of being given tetanus toxiod injections, he died of tetanus within two weeks.

A ten-day-old baby of professing Christians was brought in with stomach pains and found to have thirty-four cuts over her abdomen — to let the pain out! Then a Pakistani man was admitted in very poor shape. Gwen kept him in her own spare room to give intravenous fluids. Lily also had her spare room occupied — Comfort Udoudom was again very ill. She seemed so close to death that they were in doubt that she would survive till morning. Prayer was made for her and both Gwen and Lily felt that the Lord was indicating they should treat her for typhoid. Within a remarkably short time she responded wonderfully, and so prayer was turned to praise.

There followed a five-year-old with tetanus, who recovered; and a woman with a badly wounded foot caused by an axe missing the tree she was cutting. Gwen was glad to have her new suturing equipment to use. And so it went on, almost before she could catch her breath: emergencies, large clinics, F.C.S. meetings, domestic chores. Not much time to be homesick.

Someone had given her a new dog — "Rocky by name and softie by nature". Gwen noticed he liked a good variation in his diet. In the first few days he ate one tablecloth, one tape recorder carrier, one fly swat, one paperback, part of a mat, and one of Gwen's uniforms! This was the kind of dog to provide Gwen with many a laugh. But unhappily, his curiosity may have been his undoing, for after only a few weeks he died from a snake bite. Though this would have given Gwen considerable grief, a far weightier sorrow was soon to come.

CHAPTER 9

Proved Genuine

The small Mitsubishi minibus rocked and swayed over the pot-holed road as it headed north out of Kanyehu toward Kaduna, four hour's drive away. Inside, the two women were unusually quiet. Gwen's heart lurched with apprehension as she tried to guess the meaning behind that brief message she had received — "Phone home; urgent!" What news would greet her when she made contact with her family in London? She hardly noticed the road, or the villages and people they passed. She was wrapped in her memory of places and times which seemed to belong to another planet.

Lily too was troubled. Her thoughts were riveted on her friend. The news was hardly likely to be good and the consequences could seriously affect all concerned from London to Kanyehu. The journey seemed endless, broken only by an occasional remark. It was difficult to talk without speculation, and speculation might raise unnecessary horrors. When at last they drew into the Sudan Interior Mission Compound in Kaduna there was some relief that the mystery would soon be solved.

As Gwen sat listening to the purr of the telephone, she could visualise the hallway of the house four thousand miles away and her sister moving forward to answer. There was a click, and a familiar voice spoke clearly in her ear. First the warm greetings, then the news — as bad as Gwen's worst fears: Andrew, her beloved nephew, was dead!

When all that could be said, of consolation and regret, was finished, Gwen replaced the receiver and sank, exhausted, into a chair. She accepted with gratitude the various ministries of those who hovered around her, but her heart was far away and her mind drew vivid pictures of Andrew; the huge frame belying so gentle a nature, the slow infectious almost mischievous smile, his latest joke, his love of life for all creatures, however humble. She was torn apart to think of it all. How could such a young life be so quickly snuffed out?

She saw it all so clearly, that last short journey; his preparation to go to work, the cheery goodbye, the tall form on the motor cycle gliding away, then, so soon, came the sudden appearance of the truck overtaking on a bend, and it was all over. Andrew was killed instantly. It was Sunday, 16th September, 1984.

Questions were nagging at Gwen. She had prayed often for Andrew; had she prayed enough? As a lad he had loved the Lord; had that youthful openness led him to know the Saviour? How would Jaqui, Andrew's wife, take this terrible blow? Indeed, how would Gwen herself cope with the awful pain she was now feeling? She could think of nothing worse than this wound, for Andrew had been, to her, very special.

Lily vetoed any plan to return immediately to Kanyehu. A house on the compound was gladly offered but the Lord had an even lovelier provision arranged for his two children.

Michael Piper, a British Naval Commander, was in Kaduna teaching in the Forces Staff College. He and his wife, Sue, and daughter, Ruth were keen to meet Gwen, of whom they had heard through Valerie Luff, and through his cousin, Miss Pat Cook. Pat is the Executive Director of the Central Asian Mission, and Michael a Council member. When Gwen and Lily turned up on the doorstep of these strangers they received a welcome as warm as from family. Beds, meals and lovely fellowship, all readily given, helped to ease the stress of the day. Sue made sure their guests would stay a few days until completely rested. A new friendship began that day, springing out of the love of God; and the prayers together that evening brought deep solace to Gwen just when she needed it. She went to bed with a freer heart.

Once back at Kanyehu after the weekend, the usual quota of patients soon had Gwen and Lily deeply involved, and as the days moved into weeks the sheer necessity of so many demands was a balm to the wounds of bereavement. The joy of the Lord was Gwen's strength; she began to sing again and spice her prayers with liberal doses of praise. There was something special to anticipate too. The Pipers, Pat Cook, and her friend, Dr. Jean Mutimer, were due to come to Kanyehu for a visit. Pat and Jean had visited Val in Pakistan and were now in Nigeria at the Pipers' home. Gwen and Lily looked forward to the first weekend of December, 1984 with great delight.

Gwen was coming to the end of her twenty-eighth year in Nigeria. She and Valerie were planning to retire together after this tour. It would be great to hear first-hand news of Val from Pat and Jean. There was plenty of preparation for the invasion; cooking, cleaning and shifting of beds. Happily, they had some help from Margaret Menzies, who was in Nigeria on a short tour of voluntary help to the Qua Iboe family, and was staying at Kanyehu.

At last the day dawned, the guests arrived and a memorable weekend of laughter, fellowship and sharing began. A stream of people from church and village came and went. Problems were discussed and prayed over. Songs were sung and great gusts of merriment echoed back and forth across the compound. On a visit to the secondary school at Umaisha both Pat and Michael spoke to the F.C.S. It was bountifully apparent that the students had a special affection for Gwen and she for them.

During a meal at Kanyehu a curious thing happened. Without warning, Michael began to choke. His rasping coughing, bulging eyes and face turning rapidly bluer by the second, brought Jean to the rescue. Her technique of standing behind him and squeezing hard on his diaphragm failed to work because she was not tall enough. Pat took over and, after several tries, eventually succeeded in checking the convulsions.

Perhaps nothing more would have been thought of this if it had not been that at the very next meal, when someone turned to speak to Gwen, they found her almost asphyxiated and wholly unable to respond. Jean went into action again and Gwen recovered; but the doctor was convinced that both Michael and Gwen could well have died from suffocation.

Sue had mentioned on arrival at Kanyehu that she was aware of an atmosphere of pervading evil in the place. Now they all wondered if they were under some special attack from the enemy. They went to prayer to claim the Lord's protection.

Late on Sunday afternoon, 2nd December, the Pipers left Kanyehu for Kaduna. Gwen would follow the next day after her clinic, bringing Pat and Jean with her. Jean had particularly wanted to observe the clinic in action. Rita Paul, Gwen's Sri Lankan friend, would travel to Kaduna with them too.

On Monday over one hundred and fifty patients came for treatment. Dr. Jean was astonished at the number and variety of cases being cared for, and at Gwen's skills — much more those of a doctor than a nurse. There was surprising orderliness too, for an African group. Perhaps Jean was unaware how long it had taken Gwen to drill into her patients the need to wait their turn quietly. At times she had nearly made herself hoarse trying to keep order. At last, after years of hard work most of these people knew that Sister meant what she said and that she cared about their needs. They flocked to her, trusted her, and took note when scolded by her. She was often the only shelter for them from pain and death. She was their mother.

Finally, the clinic was over, the equipment put away ready for the next time, and, after a meal, the minibus was ready for the road. Goodbyes were said to Lily and Margaret, last minute instructions given to staff, and plans for the return, expected at the end of the week, gone over once again. Then they were off, singing and chatting their way to Kaduna.

The healthy mixture of spiritual discussion, prayer and fun enjoyed at Kanyehu continued through the week spent together in Kaduna. For Gwen it was a time of renewal and rest rarely equalled. When Friday, 7th December came, she faced the prospect of a return to Kanyehu with a new hope, a warm heart and great joy.

The minibus had been fully serviced and stood loaded at the door. Rita and Gwen said a multitude of goodbyes; there were hugs and kisses and jokes and blessings. As she stowed her handbag out of sight of thieves and bandits, Gwen pointed out the place to Pat. "They would have a job to find it there," she said with a chuckle.

The journey began; the road was good; they jogged steadily towards Kanyehu. Did they speak of the Lord? Did they sing His praises? Did they share one another's problems? It would not be unusual if they did.

At about 2 p.m. near the town of Suleja and half-way to Kanyehu, they were travelling on a newly-built tarred road when a luxury single-decker Mercedes coach approached at speed from the opposite direction. A cow was wandering on the road. When Gwen saw the bus swerve she pulled her car away to the side as far as she could go, but the huge vehicle bore down upon her and collided head-on. So great was the impact that the smaller car was slammed thirty metres back along the road it had come. Gwen and Rita died instantly.

At Kanyehu Lily Brannan and Margaret Menzies had prepared a welcome-home meal for the expected travellers. They were not over-concerned as time went on, for Africa is a land of delays. When it came to 7 p.m., however, they decided to eat. Hardly had they finished the meal when some garbled reports were brought to them that a car had been in an accident. One man who had heard the rumours offered to go back along the road to find out the truth.

Their anxiety was greatly heightened when Rita's husband arrived with students from the secondary school. They had it that Gwen was dead and Rita injured. It was not for another thirty minutes or so, that at last, the full facts were brought to them by a District Traffic Officer and a Roman Catholic priest.

The Bassa and Gwari Christians of Kanyehu came immediately to comfort the two women in their shattering loss. The care and love they showed knew no bounds. They decided that two motor cycles should go to Igala; one carrying Lily on the pillion, the other carrying Elder Jonah Zhiya.

After a night when sleep was virtually impossible, the little party set out at 4.15 a.m. on Saturday, bearing the sad news to the rest of the Qua Iboe family. The cold Harmattan wind blew strongly as they took the old cow trail which skirts the northern bank of the Benue river. By 6.30 a.m., as the eastern sky lightened, the four travellers and two machines were being paddled across the river, precariously perched on a swaying canoe. Lily's great problem was to keep warm. She had an anorak thrown over her shoulders but the lower part of her body and legs were really cold. Once on the southern shore they raced to the home of Robert and Joyce Hyslop at Odenyi.

Within minutes Robert had packed a bag and they were on the road again, this time in the Hyslops' minibus. The journey to Ochadamu was swift despite the winding rough road. The morning's work at this medical centre was under way, the staff scattered all over the vast compound which makes up the various units of the hospital, but, once Robert and Lily broke into the scene with their crushing news there was a rapid response, a coming together of kindred hearts, bearing up each other under such a wave of grief and shock.

A brief consultation, a little refreshment and there was need to move on. Lily, Robert, Graham Trice and Jonah set out for Kaduna, a long gruelling journey made the more trying by the knowledge of all that had yet to be done ere this dreadful day was through. At Kanyehu, Margaret Menzies could only wait out her lonely vigil, wondering all the while how Lily was faring.

The travellers reached Gwagwalada where the accident had actually taken place. They were informed by the police that Mr. Paul, Rita's husband, had collected items from the smashed vehicle and gone on to Suleja hospital where the bodies of Gwen and Rita lay. They followed the same route and arrived at Suleja at 8.45 p.m.

Now a very distressing situation arose. It was terrible enough to have to see their beloved Gwen as her body now was after so awful an accident, but on top of that, and the weariness of travel, they faced the callousness of the local carpenter who was determined to squeeze as much out of these bereaved strangers as he could for the rough plywood coffin he made. It was 12.30 a.m., Sunday 9th December, before the coffin was completed and at 1 a.m. the journey to Kaduna recommenced.

It would be hard to imagine how great a shock it was for Pat Cook, Jean Mutimer and the Piper family to be awakened at 3.20 that Sunday morning and be told the tragic news that they were the last of Gwen's friends to see her alive, and that within a brief two hours of her departure from this house she had gone to be with the Lord. There was hardly time, however, for the news to sink in, or to stop for anything more than a drink, before the return journey with all its attendant business, would take their full attention.

Michael checked the car, which had been playing up a little, the lights dimming ominously, on the last part of the journey. Sue found a white sheet, needles and thread to use as a shroud, and by 4.20 a.m. the minibus pulled out onto the road southward; the vanguard of a small convoy of three cars. At 6.30 a.m. they drove into the hospital grounds and were met by Noah Gadaga and other young Christian men from Kanyehu who had spent the night at Suleja watching over Gwen's body. Mr. Paul had already removed the body of his wife and returned to Umaisha.

Lily and Pat lovingly undertook the task of preparing Gwen's body for burial. Once safely sealed in the rude casket Gwen was lifted gently by reverent Bassa and Gwari men and conveyed to the waiting cars outside, to take her last journey over rough Nigerian roads, back to Kanyehu where she had lived and worked for so long. The cortege, with the customary green boughs tied on the front, stopped once, at the site of the crash.

Gwen's handbag had not been found. It contained her passport, money, watch and other important items. Pat remembered then almost the last words she had heard Gwen speak when she pointed out the bag's hiding place: "They would have a job to find it there." Michael Piper, helped by the Nigerians travelling with them, managed to free the bag from the tangled wreckage after a half-hour struggle. Everything was intact. They resumed their journey, which for Lily and Jonah had already lasted thirty hours.

When the minibus had left Ochadamu the previous afternoon the Qua Iboe family had swung into action. Preparations were made for most of the staff to go to Kanyehu for the funeral. Some had to remain behind to cover duties, and a few were not well enough to travel. The first consideration, though, was to circulate the news to Ugwolawo, Ochaja and Enweli where various folk were working. One worry was that Robert Thompson, the Senior Executive, was still not home from a trip to Jos and had no idea that this tragedy had happened. It was when he called at Ochaja later that he learned this sad news. He hurried back to Ochadamu to join the trek north again to Bassa.

About midnight on Saturday Joyce Hyslop, who had been alone all day since Robert had left so hurriedly, heard a car labouring up the gravel hill towards her house in Odenyi. She went out to meet it, and out tumbled the weary travellers. To take in so many unexpected guests so late at night would present major problems in any place, much more so in the heart of the bush country. Joyce took it all in her stride. After a fitful night and very early start the mourners left Odenyi, taking Joyce with them, crossing the Benue from Ogba to Igwa Pati by two paddle canoes. The canoes leaked freely and needed constant baling to keep the water from the passengers' feet. As they glided over the wide, gently flowing river that Sunday morning, wrapped in silent thought, the peaceful scene was in such stark contrast to the horror of the accident. The events of the past hours seemed to fade away with the mists of the river like a dream. Was it really all true?

A battered pick-up awaited their arrival on the far shore. By the time seven missionaries and the driver were wedged inside, and five Nigerians plus loads were piled on the back, the vehicle was wallowing, hardly clear of the ground. An extraordinary journey then ensued as the unfortunate truck waddled, bumped and swayed its zig-zag way in and out of huge potholes, down stream banks, through rivers and, groaning pathetically, chugged up the sandy hills. Had it not been for the solemn nature of this particular journey, the whole experience would have been, in Gwen's words, "a hoot". Certainly, she would have enjoyed it immensely.

Their route took them past the spot where the pioneers of the early 1900s had their graves. Thoughts turned to the scriptures: "Except a corn of wheat fall into the ground and die it abides alone, but if it die it brings forth much fruit." And again: "Precious in the sight of the Lord is the death of His saints."

Now a second party was on its way across the river. These would have to wait till the overworked pick-up could return from its thirty-mile round trip to take them over the same treacherous route. The early mists had been dispersed, as the sun climbed steadily to its zenith, gaining all the while in its tropical malevolence.

At Kanyehu the hours ticked by so very slowly for the lonely white woman. Margaret Menzies strained to hear each approaching vehicle. "Would it turn in, or just go on by?" "When would someone come to relieve her of this terrible burden of suspense?" The only sound was of subdued voices, and the "chip chip" of tools hacking at the rocky ground to make a grave. At last, around eleven on that Sunday morning, 9th December, 1984, her lonely vigil came to an end. Suddenly, her friends from Igala were there, coming towards her from the cars. She leaned wearily against the door-post, unable to walk forward to meet them.

There were hugs and soft tears as warm consolation flowed from one to another; quiet confirmation of this item, or that, of the happenings of the past two distressing days; the supply of simple refreshments for all and an hour went by. They heard a convoy approaching: it was the funeral cortege, flanked and followed by a multitude of men and women streaming towards the mission centre. Then the whole place swarmed with people of varied cultures, languages and colours merging into one, joined by a common sorrow, a common loss, and, for most, a common comfort in one Father.

Whilst the arrival of the final group of missionaries from Igala was awaited, the women's choir began to sing their rhythmic songs of praise and worship, bringing an atmosphere charged with powerful emotion. The wait was long, almost three hours, but the women sang on throughout the whole of that time. When at last they came, the throng of people moved forward to the graveside. It was three in the afternoon.

CHAPTER 10

Result in Glory

Quietly, tenderly, strong arms lifted the coffin, bearing its contents of such precious memory, and laid it at the side of the neatly dug grave. It seemed to be the place of God's choice, just in front of the old house Gwen had used when first she arrived in Kanyehu, and not far from the present health centre in which she had worked to save lives.

Noah Gadaga called the people to worship and the aged elder Jonathan opened the service with prayer. Several Nigerians spoke movingly in great appreciation of Gwen's dedicated life and work. John Atabo shared a conversation he had once had with Gwen: "I asked her," he said, "why she had not married."

She replied, "Because if I married I could not live entirely for Jesus; I want to serve Him alone."

Jonah Zhiya made the point that Gwen was really a "black woman" for she had been so long with them. Norah Curran spoke of the many years she had known Gwen as a friend and colleague.

It was then that an unexpected note of humour slipped into the proceedings. Dr. Derek Belgrave was to speak, but the announcement was confused to Dr. Billy Graham (Bel-grave sounding somewhat similar to the African ear). A correction was made, but without success, Dr. Billy Graham was again announced! There were sly smiles and glances between the assembled Europeans. Almost all had the same thought, "How Gwen would have loved it and laughed long and hard." It was almost as if she were giving them all a nudge not to be so solemn on her account.

Among the many Christians were a sprinkling of Moslems listening intently to the Word of God preached by Derek and Robert Hyslop. One man, the Paramount Chief of Umaisha, had left his civic responsibilities at the annual Gani Festival to be at the service — a great honour and a sure sign of his appreciation of Gwen and the medical work at Kanyehu.

Barely a week before her death Gwen had mentioned that she would like the hymn "Thine be the glory", sung at her funeral. This was not in the local hymnbooks, so her white friends got together and sang it from memory. To those Nigerians present for whom English is totally unknown, the grandly triumphant music and the faces of the singers would have conveyed almost the whole message of the song of glory to God, whose victory over death is indeed endless.

Slowly and reverently, black and white hands together, lowered the coffin into its final place. A ledge had been cut just clear of the casket on which now were laid a series of branches, then sheets of corrugated iron were placed on top of the wood before the whole was then covered with earth — the soil of Bassa in which Gwen was firmly planted in hope of a mighty harvest.

Many owed their lives, or that of their children, to Gwen's patient skill as a nurse. Some owed their spiritual lives to Gwen's witness to the Saviour she loved. Many shared in the sunshine she radiated through her infectious faith and laughter. All around that grave had been touched by an extraordinary life and, to some extent, would never be the same again. One Kanyehu woman, knowing that Gwen was serving her last tour before retirement said, 'We did not want her to go home. Now she will be with us for ever."

One of the Bassa elders pleaded for someone to be sent to take Gwen's place. Gwen herself, when faced with complicated medical problems, had often sighed, "If only we had a doctor here." Within a few weeks Dr. Roy Jones and his wife, Jane, moved to Kanyehu with their youngest child — the other two being sent to school in Jos, four hours' drive away. Like their Master, like the early pioneers, like Gwen, they were ready to step out on that path of faith and sacrifice which brings the exquisite mixture of pain and joy, discouragement and delight, fear and hope, known only to those who are His disciples. These, with their brothers and sisters in Christ scattered through the generations of the past and the world of the present, learn at last to say with joy: "When He has tried me I shall come forth as gold."

SYON MISSION CHURCH, LONDON
12th JANUARY, 1985
SERVICE OF THANKSGIVING FOR
GWEN GOLD

Tears flowed freely down the young woman's cheeks. Her closed eyes were directed Godward in devotion as she sang. The powerful emotions chasing over her face reflected the deep current stirring every one of the two hundred people present. Sorrow at the loss of one so loved, joy at the certain knowledge that that one was now with the Lord, and compassion for the bereaved, all served to melt hearts into a bond of unity.

As the Thanksgiving Service progressed the element of joy swelled, overriding the natural sorrow, to the point where laughter often broke through and consolation was found in the Lord, His Word, and even in His inscrutable purposes. Those who were to take part in this special service wondered how they could freely open their thoughts to all without being swept into feelings too strong to control; but Valerie Luff, who spoke first, and might have had most cause to dissolve, was given grace to speak of her closest friend with warm delight and positive faith.

As the several speakers shared their memories, so the pattern took shape from early days of faith and training, to service in various areas of Nigeria, and right on to the point of Gwen's departure into the arms of her Beloved. The solo, "There's a sound on the wind," seemed to ring back from heaven a song of victory and encouragement to those who remain — "Come on, Heaven's children, the city is in sight". Indeed, the 'veil between' seemed transparent, mingling earth with heaven as though it were all one.

Pastor Herbert brought the meeting to a fitting climax in his brief address:

> It is natural to ask, "Why?" but to this question we may not find an answer. The question we should ask is, "What?" What does God want me to learn from this seeming tragedy? What are His purposes for the future of His work in Bassa? What part am I to play in that work?

Of all the songs we sang, some poignant with memories, others swelling with faith, one in particular caught an echo from the voices of friends who so recently had stood beside a grave in Kanyehu singing "Thine be the Glory, risen conquering Son, Endless is the Victory Thou, o'er death, hast won."

The meeting over, many were reluctant to break away from fellowship, and the warmth continued over refreshments and comments on the various aspects of the evening. One very special blessing flowed from the way the Qua Iboe Fellowship and the Central Asian Mission had been drawn together around a shared tragedy and triumph. Pat Cook and Jean Mutimer were witnesses to the last days of Gwen's life as well as key helpers in her funeral arrangements. Valerie Luff, so deeply affected, had flown home from Pakistan to be at this event. The reality of our unity of purpose in the worldwide proclamation of the gospel, our oneness in the bonds of Christ's love, and our common involvement in Gwen's life, all combined to weld us together in a way that was positively precious.

Then there was the church itself at Syon, and its pastor, whose support of Gwen throughout her missionary service had been constant, thoughtful and effective. Now, giving all to arrange this service, and cater for the needs of visitors, from as far afield as Scotland, Ulster, Wiltshire and Birmingham, they excelled again. Missions, whose overseas staff are supported by their home churches in prayer, interest, finance and pastoral care to the extent that Gwen Gold was, soon come to appreciate the great value of this to all concerned.

The final sentences on Gwen's last prayer letter, written just before her death, stated, "Please accept my greetings (for Christmas 1984) with this letter. I trust you will have as happy a time as I expect to have." Gwen spent her Christmas in the presence of the Christ of Christmas, experiencing a joy which is far beyond anything she might have known on earth; a joy which, for her, will never be interrupted, and for us is yet to be.